MADRAS GOVERNMENT MUSEUM BULLETIN
VOL. I, NO. 4.
ANTHROPOLOGY

TODAS AND KOTAS OF THE NILGIRI HILLS AND OF THE BRAHMANS, KAMMALANS, PALLIS AND PARIAHS OF MADRAS CITY

MADRAS GOVERNMENT MUSEUM BULLETIN
VOL. I, NO. 4.
ANTHROPOLOGY

TODAS AND KOTAS OF THE NILGIRI HILLS AND OF THE BRAHMANS, KAMMALANS, PALLIS AND PARIAHS OF MADRAS CITY

EDGAR THURSTON

WITH EIGHTEEN PLATES

GYAN

Published by

GYAN

Gyan Publishing House
5, Ansari Road
Daryaganj, New Delhi-110002
Phone: 011-47034999, 9811692060
E-mail: books@gyanbooks.com

Distribution Network
gyanbooks.com
India, USA, Canada, UK, Australia, France

ISBN : 978-81-212-4125-0 (PB)
First Published, 1896

2nd Impression 2020

Printed at: Gyan Press, Delhi.

Todas and Kotas of the Nilgiri Hills
Author: Edgar Thurston

MADRAS GOVERNMENT MUSEUM.

Bulletin No. 4.

ANTHROPOLOGY

OF THE

TODAS AND KOTAS OF THE NILGIRI HILLS

AND OF THE

BRÁHMANS, KAMMÁLANS, PALLIS, AND PARIAHS OF MADRAS CITY.

BY

EDGAR THURSTON, C.M.Z.S., ETC.,
Superintendent Madras Government Museum.

MADRAS:
PRINTED BY THE SUPERINTENDENT, GOVERNMENT PRESS.

1896.

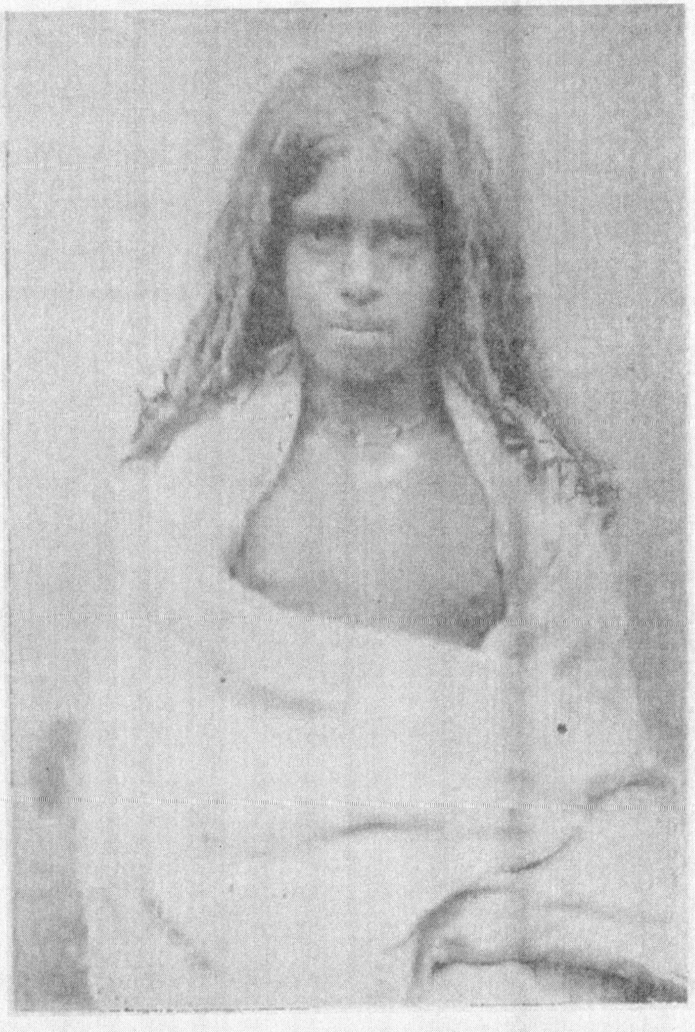

A TODA BEAUTY

E. THURSTON PHOT.

PHOTO-PRINT SURVEY OFFICE, MADR
1895.

THE TODAS OF THE NILGIRIS.

A CURIOUS people are the Todas or Tudas, to whom the most sacred objects on this earth are a holy dairy-man (pālāl) and a large-horned race of semi-domesticated buffaloes, on whose milk and the products thereof (butter and ney [1]) they still depend largely, though to a less extent than in bygone days, before the existence of the Ootacamund bazár, for subsistence.

Their origin is, in the absence of any except very vague tradition connecting them with Rāma or Rāvana, and of written language, veiled in obscurity, but they take it on trust, without displaying any interest in the matter, that they are the original inhabitants of the Nilgiris, on which they have dwelt from time immemorial. "So," they say, "our grandfathers told us. How can we know otherwise?"

Being myself no philologist, I must rest content with merely recording, without criticism, the different views which have been pronounced as to the origin of the Toda language. According to Dr. Pope, it seems to have been originally old Kanarese, and not a distinct dialect. Dr. Caldwell held, on the other hand, to the view that, of all the Dravidian idioms, Tamil is that to which the Toda language is most nearly allied; and the German missionary Metz found at least eighty out of a hundred words commonly made use of by a Toda to be indentical with, or derived from, words used by their Dravidian neighbours, and thought that the language is most nearly connected with old Kanarese.

According to Dr. Oppert, the latest philological writer on the races of Southern India,[2] the Todas are of Turanian or Scythian descent, and there is no doubt but that they belong to the Gaudian branch of the Gauda-Dravidian group, whose settlements got flooded out by successive waves of the Aryan invasion. If this theory be true, the Todas were originally mountaineers, even if, as Dr. Oppert says, they ascended from the plains to the Nilgiri Hills. In support of the origin of their name from Koda or Kuda, signifying

[1] Ney=ghi or clarified butter.
[2] The Original Inhabitants of India, 1893.

a mountaineer, he records that, when inquiring into their name, he was informed by various natives, and even by some Todas, that the Todavar are also called Kodavar. This statement is, however, not borne out by the replies to my repeated inquiries in search of confirmation thereof. Todavar the Todas admit, but they will not hear of their being called Kodavar, despite the fact that there is a Toda mand at Kodanād on the eastern side of the Nilgiris.

According to Colonel Marshall, whose 'Phrenologist among the Todas' (1873) should be read by any who are interested in the tribe, "there is much of the 'blameless Ethiopian' about them: something of the Jew and of the Chaldæan in their appearance."

An attempt has been made to connect the Todas with the lost tribes, and, amid a crowd of Todas assembled together to celebrate a funeral rite, there is no difficulty in picking out many individuals, whose features would find for them a ready place as actors on the Ober Amergau stage, either in leading or subordinate parts.

Clothed and without arms, the Todas for the most part lead a simple pastoral life, comparatively little influenced by the presence of Europeans in their midst. Female infanticide, which was formerly practised to a wide extent, has, however, entirely ceased under British rule. There can, I think, be no doubt that Toda infanticide must be attributed to a desire to keep down the population, and not, as has been suggested, to a desire felt by the women to retain their good looks, which rapidly disappear, whether the babies are killed or no. "I don't know," said an elderly Toda to Colonel Marshall, "whether it was wrong or not to kill them, but we were very poor, and could not support our children. Now every one has a mantle (putkūli), but formerly there was only one for the whole family, and he who had to go out took the mantle, the rest remaining at home naked all but the loin cloth (kuvn)." Polyandry is, in consequence of the larger number of females who now grow up and become available for matrimonial purposes, on the decline, and resorted to only by the poorer class of Todas, who have not the means to support a separate married establishment. Of polyandry the Todas are at heart ashamed, and strenuously deny its existence until hard pressed. The Ootacamund Todas assured me that in their mands no cases of polyandry existed, but that it was practised by the 'jungle Todas' at Paikāra. But, during my stay at Paikāra, I was quite as strongly assured that no woman of the neighbouring mands

PL. VIII

TODA MAN

E. THURSTON PHOT.

PHOTO-PRINT SURVEY OFFICE, MADRAS.
1895.

had more than one husband, though polyandry prevailed at Ootacamund.

In the system of polyandry as practised by the Todas, if one of several brothers is married to a woman, the other brothers may, as my interpreter expressed it, 'enjoy privileges'; or, if a man's wife has one or more younger sisters, they may become wives of their sister's husband or husbands —an arrangement which complicates relationship. In lieu of a no-admission card or 'not-at-home' box, a walking stick and mantle (putkūli) are placed outside the door of the hut as an indication that one of the men is with the woman, and entrance into the hut is forbidden.

During the last quarter of a century the number of Todas, both male and female, has increased to a slight extent, as shown by the following tabular statement based on the census figures of 1871, 1881, and 1891 :—

Year.	Males.	Females.	Total.
1871	405	288	693
1881	380	293	673
1891	424	312	736
Increase ...	19	24	43

Writing in 1868, Dr. Shortt in his 'Account of the tribes of the Nilgiris,' makes a sweeping assertion that "most of their women have been debauched by Europeans, who, it is sad to observe, have introduced diseases, to which these innocent tribes were at one time perfect strangers, and which, as they have no means of curing, are slowly, but no less surely sapping their once hardy and vigorous constitutions. The effects of intemperance and disease (syphilis) combined are becoming more and more apparent in the shaken and decrepit appearance, which at the present day these tribes generally present." Fact it undoubtedly is, and proved both by hospital and naked-eye evidence, that syphilis has been introduced among the Todas, as among the Andamanese, by contact with more civilised races. Fact it also undoubtedly is, notwithstanding Colonel Marshall's phrenological belief that the necessity for stimulants is a property of the brachycephalic head, that the dolichocephalic Toda displays a marked partiality for gin, port, bottled beer and arrack, and will willingly drink neat brandy in a mug; and the silver coins given, with cheroots, as a bribe to induce subjects to come and have their measurements recorded at my improvised laboratory, were expended entirely on drink in the bazár. But I have never seen a Toda, as I have repeatedly seen Kotas and Badagas, staggering homeward from the drink shops in the bazár in a disgusting state of brawling intoxication, or, in fact, much the worse for drink. Nor would any one who has studied them regard the Todas otherwise than as a hardy race, of fine physique, and, in the case of the women, modestly behaved (with an occasional exception of solicitation) in the presence of Europeans, despite the oft-repeated statement that "the women show an absence of any sense of decency or indecency in exposing their naked persons in the presence of strangers."

Morality, it must be confessed, is reduced to a very low ebb previous to marriage—a civil contract which is regarded as binding, and acts, in some measure, as a check to irregular intercourse. And, it must also be confessed, the Toda has not a strict regard for truth, when any advantage is to be derived from telling a falsehood. As an example of mild Toda mendacity the following incident may be quoted. Instructions had been issued for a girl aged ten to be brought to me to be measured and photographed. On the following day a damsel was accordingly produced, who was stated to be ten years old, and not to have reached puberty. She was well developed, with the measurements of a young adult; possessed a well marked moustache; and was tattooed, as if she was a married woman, on the chest, hand, legs and feet. It was explained to me that the girl and a friend had tattooed each other as a joke. I attributed the story of her age and the origin of the tattoo marks to mendacity with a view to the receipt of the customary baksheesh; and it subsequently turned out that the girl was at least eighteen years old, had been married some years previously and divorced for immorality, and was about to marry a second husband undaunted by her previous life history. In the case just cited the age was wilfully misrepresented; but, as a matter of fact, the Todas have very little idea of age after they are grown up. A little cross questioning would at times bring the subject's age down, *e.g.*, from seventy to fifty, recalling to mind the story of the Native who remarked: "This year my father is sixty-eight. Next year he will be one hundred and eight."

TODA WOMAN

I. THURSTON PHOT. PHOTO-PRINT SURVEY OFFICE, MADRAS.
1895.

In the course of my wanderings I met with more than one man who had served, or was still serving, Government in the modest capacity of a forest guard; and I have heard of others who have been employed, not with conspicuous success, on planter's estates. In connection with the objection of the Todas to work, it is recorded that when, on one occasion, a mistake about the ownership of some buffaloes committed an old Toda to jail, it was found impossible to induce him to work with the convicts, and the authorities, unwilling to resort to hard measures, were compelled to save appearances by making him an overseer.

At the present day the Nilgiri C.M.S. Tamil Mission has extended its sphere of work to the Todas, and I cannot resist the temptation to narrate the Toda version of the story of Dives and Lazarus, with its moral, as given, I believe, to a missionary lady on the occasion of an examination. The English say that once upon a time a rich man and a poor man died. At the funeral of the rich man there was a great tamásha, and many buffaloes were sacrificed. But for the funeral of the poor man neither music nor buffaloes were provided. The English believe that in the next world the poor man was as well off as the rich man, so that, when any one dies, it is of no use spending money on the funeral ceremonies.

Two schools have been established, one at Ootacamund, the other near Paikāra. It is said that, in their yearly migration to distant mands for change of pasture for their herds, some of the Todas leave their children behind at the mands near the schools, with some one to take care of them, in order that their lessons may not be interrupted. No Toda, I was informed, has as yet been baptised.

A Toda 'conductor,' who receives a small monthly salary, and capitation allowance for every child who attends school regularly, showed us the way to the Paikāra school, where eighteen children (sixteen boys and two girls), varying in age from seven to sixteen, and some clad in ill-fitting jackets instead of the picturesque putkūli, were reading elementary Tamil and English, and doing simple arithmetic. One boy, a bright and intelligent lad, aged twelve, was working for the 'third standard,' and read English very fairly, but with artificial Hindu intonation instead of the natural musical Toda voice. I could not help wondering whether this lad will be content, as he grows up, to live the simple life of a Toda herdsman, or will enter into the lists in the struggle for a small-paid appointment under

Government. The Toda is even now, as I have experienced, capable of submitting petitions, written in the bazár, 'begging your honour,' etc.; and it is to be feared, from an ethnographic standpoint, that the spread of education among them will tend to obliterate that spirit of independence and simplicity of character which have hitherto distinguished the Todas favourably from the other inhabitants of Southern India. A quarter of a century ago the Todas are said to have had "just so much knowledge of the speech of their vassals as is demanded by the most ordinary requirements";[3] whereas, at the present day, a few write, and many converse fluently in Tamil. One man I came across, who, with several other Todas, was selected on account of fine physique for exhibition at Barnum's show in Europe, America, and Australia some years ago, and still retained a smattering of English, talking fondly of 'Shumbu' (the elephant Jumbo). For some time after his return to his hill abode, a tall white hat (cylinder-hut) was the admiration of his fellow tribesmen. To this man finger prints came as no novelty, as his impressions were recorded both in England and America.

Characteristics.

A self-possessed and cheery person is the Toda, and fully capable of appreciating a joke. The appearance of a European (who is greeted as swāmi) in a mand is a signal for a general cry among the inhabitants, male and female, for inām (alms), not so much because they are professional mendicants, as because experience has taught them that visitors generally disgorge small sums, and, like the Father of the Marshalsea, they make capital out of human weakness. As a rule, they have no objection to Europeans entering into their huts, but on one occasion we were politely requested to take off our boots before crawling in on our stomachs, so as not to desecrate "the deep recesses of their odorous dwelling."

The friendly disposition of the Todas towards Europeans is well brought out by the following note, with which a former forest-settlement officer of the Nilgiris has been good enough to supply me. "Bickapathi mand, or, as Tommy Atkins from Wellington dubs it, Pick-pack mand, is one of the most picturesque. It is situated on the top of a grand saddle, and furnishes a magnificent view of the Mysore ditch and the grand teak forests beyond. I had frequent occasion to go there, and soon got on friendly

---

[3] W. Ross King—*The Aboriginal Tribes of the Nilgiri Hills.*

terms with the Todas, whose ladies greatly appreciated the bazár-made sweetmeats of Ootacamund, and whose men—Toda-like—were always ready to accept the seeds of garden vegetables given to them by the forest officer, so long as a Badaga did all the digging, weeding and bedding, at our expense. One bright little girl, aged about eight, used to sing to us in the evening a Tamil song, which she had picked up from a C.M.S. Missionary, the refrain of which, 'Thēvan nallavan' (God is good), chanted in her quaint crooning little voice, still runs in my head. Meantime her brother, a good-looking picturesque lad aged ten, would wait expectantly by, watching with wistful eye until the expected piece of chocolate, fig, biscuit, or other delicacy, was forthcoming.

"One night, while we were encamped hard by, a tiger, or possibly a pair of them, stampeded the buffaloes out of the kraal close to the mand, and killed no less than six of them, as they blindly fled for a couple of miles over almost impassable country. It was my good fortune a few days later to come across, stalk in the open, and shoot this tiger. Nor was this all, for, on the following day, I shot close to the mand a sāmbar stag (*Cervus unicolor*). In a space of twenty-four hours I had thus ridded the mand of their dreaded enemy the tiger, and got for its inhabitants a surfeit of the only flesh that Todas are allowed to eat. This was too great an occasion to be passed over in silence, or to be treated with ordinary formalities. Something special was called for, and the Todas, to a man and woman, rose to the occasion. A new and original ode, in which I, and not the evergreen Rāman, was the hero, was improvised. The Todas from the neighbouring mands were hastily summoned; a dress rehearsal was held at mid-day; and in the evening a friend and I were treated to the serenade. I wish I had a copy of the ode. Its fine dithyrambic periods reminded us of Pindar in his loftiest moments. The whole available musical talent of the mand was requisitioned, and, as we sat beneath the clear canopy of a star-decked sky, we felt the performance was one worth going miles to see and hear."

The typical Toda man is above medium height, well proportioned and stalwart, with straight nose, regular features, and perfect teeth. In some instances the expression is of a conspicuously Jewish type, but, as Colonel Ross King points out [4] "the general contour of the head and cast of

[4] *Op. cit.*

countenance are rather such as we are accustomed to associate with the ancient Roman;" and their outer garment (putkūli) of thick cotton cloth with red and blue stripes woven into it, which reaches from the shoulders to the knees, hanging in graceful folds, with one end flung over the left shoulder, is commonly (and wrongly) compared to the Roman toga.

The principal characteristic, which at once distinguishes the Todas from the other tribes of the Nilgiris, is the development of the pilous (hairy) system. This characteristic, as well as the projecting superciliary arches, and dolichocephalic skull, the Toda man possesses in common with the Australians and the Ainus, but it sinks into insignificance before the remarkable hairy development represented in Mr. Savage Landor's illustration of his lunatic Ainu friend. Occasionally, as my notes record, the hair is feebly developed on the chest; but only in one case—that of a man aged fifty—out of the large number which I have examined, have I observed a marked arrest of development of the hairy system (pl. XVIII). The hair of the head was in this case short, and not bushy; beard, whiskers and moustache were represented by light down, and gave the man the appearance of a professional actor. There was an absence of hair on the chest and abdomen; a few stray hairs in the armpits, no hair on the back and upper arms; and only feebly-developed hair on the extensor surface of the fore-arms and lower extremities.

The odour of the person of the Todas, caused, I imagine, by the rancid butter which they apply to their cloths as a preservative agent, is quite characteristic, and furnishes a differential character. The missionary Huc declared that he could recognise the Negro, Tartar, Thibetan, Hindu and Chinese by their effluvium; and, with a view to testing his sense of smell, long after our return from the Nilgiris, I blindfolded a friend, who had accompanied me on my Toda campaign, and presented before his nose a cloth, which he at once recognised as having something to do with the Todas by its strong and characteristic odour.

As a type of a Toda man in many points, though considerably below the average height, the following case may be cited:—

1. Male, aged 40. Owns twenty buffaloes; makes ney from the milk, and sells it in the Ootacamund bazár. With the proceeds purchases rice, salt, chillies, tamarinds, saffron,

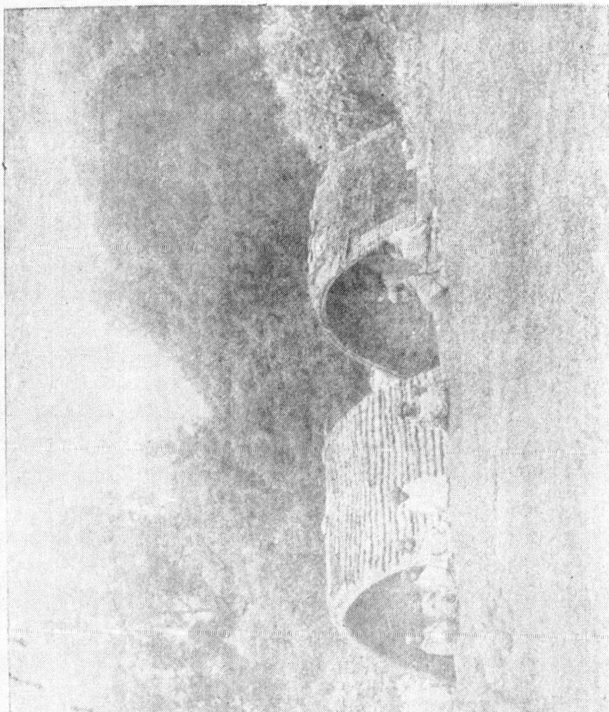

TODA MAND.

potatoes, brinjals (the fruit of *Solanum melongena*), etc. Does not as a rule eat meat, but says that he would have no objection to eating the flesh of sambar (*Cervus unicolor*). Drinks arrack, gin, bottled beer, etc.

Height 159·2 cm.

Weight 98 lbs.

Skin dirty copper brown, much darker than that of the surrounding females.

Hair black, with stray grey hairs on head, face, chest and shoulders. Beard luxuriant. Hair of head parted in middle, and hanging in curls over forehead and back of neck. Hair thickly developed on chest and abdomen, with median strip of dense hairs on the latter. Hair thick over upper and lower ends of scapulæ (shoulder blades), thinner over rest of back; well developed on extensor surface of upper arms, and both surfaces of fore-arms; very thick on extensor surfaces of the latter. Hair abundant on both surfaces of legs; thickest on outer side of thighs and round patella (knee-cap). Dense beard-like mass of hair beneath gluteal region (buttocks).

Face much corrugated. Length from vertex to chin 20·1 cm. Bizygomatic breadth 12·6 cm. Bigoniac breadth 9·3 cm. Glabella indistinct. Superciliary ridges very prominent. Eyebrows united across middle line by thick tuft of hairs. Cheek-bones not prominent. Lips medium, somewhat everted, not prognathous. Facial angle (of Cuvier) 67°. Teeth pearly white, entire, large, and regular.

Eyes horizontal. Iris light-brown. Incipient arcus senilis.[5] Conjunctivæ injected (this is unusual). Upper eyelid not thick; does not partially cover caruncle.[6]

Nose of semitic type. Bridge well defined. Height 5·3 cm.; breadth 3·5 cm. Nostrils wide; 2 cm. in length.

Ears not outstanding. Points well developed. Lobules detached, and pierced. Ear 5·8 cm. in length.

Cephalic length 20 cm. (the longest measurement recorded); breadth 14·6 cm.

Chest 81 cm. in circumference.

Shoulders 38·5 cm.

Hand, length 18 cm.; breadth 8·3 cm. Length of middle finger 11·7 cm. Nails of left hand kept very

---

[5] Arcus senilis is a ring of fatty degeneration in the peripheral zone of the cornea.

[6] In a very few cases the upper eyelid was noticed partially covering the caruncle.

long for combing and scratching hair. Fingers broad; nails square. Two brass rings on right little finger; two steel rings on left ring finger, and one steel ring on left little finger.

(*Note.*—The Toda men do not indulge in jewelry to the same extent as the Kotas.)

Foot, length 25·3 cm.; max: breadth 9·3 cm.

The average height of the Toda man, according to my measurements, is 169·6 cm., but one of the men who were selected for exhibition at Barnum's show, was 179 cm. high, and at a funeral ceremony I picked out a man towering above every one else, whose measurements were as follows:—

2. Man, aged 25. Pigeon breasted.
Height 185 cm. Record by 6 cm.
Chest 84·5 cm.
Shoulders 40·5 cm.
Grande envergure (span of arms), 194 cm. Record by 5·2 cm.
Cubit, 53·2 cm. Record by 2·9 cm.
Hand, length 20 cm.; breadth 8·8 cm.
Middle finger, length 12·9 cm. Record by ·2 cm.
Hips, 29 cm.
Foot, length 27·4 cm.; max: breadth 9·5 cm.

3. The strongest man whom I came across was an elderly monegar (head-man) of venerable appearance, wearing a turban in virtue of his position. His teeth were entire, and sound, indicating the enjoyment of good digestion. The upper eyelid partially covered the caruncle. There was a preponderance of white hair on the head and face; snow white hair on the chest; and black hair on the back, arms, abdomen, and legs. His measurements, as compared with the Toda average, are herewith recorded:—

	Monegar aged 50–55.	Toda average.
Dynamometer	112 lbs.	79 lbs.
Height	175 cm.	169·6 cm.
Span of arms	179 „	175 „
Shoulders	39·5 „	39·3 „
Chest	93 „	83 „
Biceps (circumference)	32 „	..
Cubit	48·6 „	47 „
Hand, length	19·8 „	18·8 „
„ breadth	8·2 „	8·1 „
Middle finger	12·5 „	12 „
Hips	29·4 „	25·7 „

	Monegar aged 50–55.	Toda average.
Thigh (circumference).. ..	53·5 cm.	..
Calf (circumference)	34·5 ,,	..
Foot, length	26·4 ,,	26·2 cm.
,, breadth	10·1 ,,	9·2 ,,
Cephalic length	19·5 ,,	19·4 ,,
,, breadth	15 ,,	14·2 ,,
Nasal height	5·5 ,,	4·7 ,,
,, breadth	4·1 ,,	3·6 ,,
Bigoniac	10·5 ,,	9·6 ,,
Bizygomatic	13·6 ,,	12·7 ,,

As examples of Toda men who had reached advanced years, the two following were selected for record :—

4. Old man, who maintains that he is a centenarian. Bowed with age. Face wrinkled, and furrowed like a shrivelled apple. Teeth entire, but upper incisors and canines reduced to mere pegs. Says that he remembers, when he was a lad, sixty or seventy years ago, going to a great gathering of Todas at the house of Mr. Sullivan (one of the first Europeans who visited the Nilgiris), who explained to them that the Government was paternally inclined towards them.

5. Man said to be sixty years old, but looks many years older. Bowed with age. Face wrinkled and furrowed. Advanced arcus senilis. Teeth entire, and in good condition. Muscles wasted and flabby.

Hair of head long and wavy, white with scattered tufts of black. Moustache and beard white, with diffused black hairs. Eye-brows black with scattered white hairs; united across middle line by black and white hairs curving upwards. Hair on chest and shoulders white; on abdomen black with sparse white hairs. White hair on back above spine of scapula; black hairs over body of scapula; and below inferior angle. Extensor surface of upper extremities very hairy. Preponderance of black hairs on upper arm, and white on fore-arm. Abundant black hair in armpits. Legs very hairy on both extensor and flexor surfaces. Preponderance of white hair on front and outer side of upper leg. Black, with scattered white hairs, on back of upper leg, and both surfaces of lower leg.

6. Man. A dense growth of long straight hairs directed outwards on helix of both ears, bearing a striking resemblance to the hairy development on the helix of the common Madras bonnet monkey (*Macacus sinicus*).

The two following cases of young lads are not, for obvious reasons, included in the table of measurements, but I place them on record as they are characteristic :—

7. Boy, aged 12. Shock head of hair. Down on upper lip. No hairy development on body. (Hair, it is said, develops between the fourteenth and seventeenth years.) Wears steel bangle round right ankle. Learning Tamil, English, and simple arithmetic, etc., at Paikāra school.

Height 143·8 cm.
Chest 68·5 cm.
Shoulders 32·7 cm.
Foot, length 23·4 cm. ; max : breadth 8·3 cm.

8. Boy, aged 16. Hair of head black, long, and wavy. Long hairs directed upwards between bushy eye-brows. Down on upper lip, and hair developing on chin, not on body. Ears pierced.

Height 156 cm.
Weight 91·5 lb.
Shoulders 34·2 cm.
Chest 76 cm.
Cubit 44·5 cm.
Hand, length 17·5 cm. ; breadth 7·7 cm.
Hips 23·1 cm.
Foot, length 25·7 cm. ; max : breadth 18·7 cm.
Cephalic length 18·7 cm.
,, breadth 14·1 cm.
Nasal height 4·5 cm.
,, breadth 3·5 cm.
Bigoniac 9·2 cm.
Bizygomatic 12·3 cm.

The Toda women are much lighter in colour than the men, and the colour of the body has been aptly described as being of a *café-au-lait* tint, and the face a shade darker. The skin of the female children and young adults is often of a warm copper hue. Some of the young women, with their hair dressed in glossy ringlets, bright, glistening eyes, and white teeth, are distinctly good-looking (frontispiece) though the face is spoiled by the lips and mouth ; but both good looks and complexion are short-lived, and the women speedily degenerate into uncomely hags.

The female outer garment consists of a robe similar to that of the men, but worn differently, being thrown over both shoulders and clasped in front by the hand.

TODA MONEGAR.

The leading characteristics of the female sex, the system of tattooing, and decoration with ornaments, are summed up in the following descriptive cases :—

9. Girl, aged 17. Father Todi ; married to a Kenna. One child (female) seven months old. A bright, good-looking, intelligent girl, of modest demeanour. Can read and write Tamil to a limited extent. Not tattooed.

Height 155 cm.

Weight 91 lbs.

Skin of a uniform warm copper hue, smooth, and dry. She looks very fair when contrasted with the surrounding men.

Hair black, parted in the middle, and worn in flowing ringlets, which fall over the shoulders and neck. Hair uniformly distributed, not tufted. Uses ghî (clarified butter) as pomatum. Possesses a looking glass. Either curls her hair herself, or gets a friend to do it.

Fine light hairs on back between shoulders, and on extensor surface of fore-arm.

Cephalic length 18·6 cm.; breadth 13·5 cm.

Face long, oval. Length from vertex to chin 20 cm. Bizygomatic 11·7 cm. Bigoniac 9·5 cm. Glabella smooth ; superciliary ridges not pronounced. Chin round. Cheek bones not prominent. Lips medium, slightly everted. Not prognathous. Facial angle 69·5. Teeth white, and well shaped.

Eyes glistening, horizontal. Iris dark brown. Conjunctivæ clear, not injected. Long, black, silky eye-lashes.

Nose straight. Height 3·7 cm. ; breadth 3·1 cm.

Ears not outstanding. Points well developed. Length 6 cm. Lobes detached, pierced and plugged with wood. Wears gold ear-rings on festive occasions.

Shoulders 34 cm.

Fingers delicate, tapering. Nails almond-shaped. Length of hand 17 cm. ; breadth 7·5 cm. Length of middle finger 10·8 cm.

Foot well shaped. Length 23 cm. ; max : breadth 8·2 cm.

Baby (named Latchmi) shaved on back part of top of head. Hair brought forward over forehead. Has round neck a silver chain in three strands, ornamented with current two-anna pieces and Arcot four-anna pieces.

10. Woman, aged 22. Sister of No. 1. Strong family likeness. Father and husband both Todis. Married between four and five years. One child (female), aged nine

months. Tattooed with three dots on back of left hand. Complexion dirty copper colour.

Hairs between shoulders, on extensor surface of upper and fore-arms, and legs. Wears silver necklet, ornamented with Arcot two-anna pieces; thread and silver armlets ornamented with cowry shells (*Cypræa moneta*) on right upper arm; thread armlet ornamented with cowries on left upper arm; glass bead bracelet on left fore-arm; brass ring on left ring finger; silver rings on right middle and ring fingers.

Lobules of ear attached, pierced. Ear-rings removed owing to grandmother's death.

11. Woman, aged 28, past her prime. Father a Kuttan; husband a Kenna. Three children (girls), of whom two are alive, aged eleven and eight.

Tattooed with a single dot on chin; rings and dots on chest (pl. XII, 2) outer side of upper arms (pl. XII, 3) back of left hand, below calves (pl. XII, 4) above ankles (pl. XII, 6) and across dorsum of feet (pl. XII, 5).

Wears thread armlet ornamented with young cowries on right fore-arm; thread armlet and two heavy ornamental brass armlets on left upper arm; ornamental brass bangle, and glass bead bracelet on left wrist; brass ring on left little finger; two steel rings on left ring finger; bead necklet ornamented with cowries.

12. Woman, aged 35. Father a Todi; husband a Pekkan. Five children (3 boys, 2 girls), all alive; youngest three years old. Tattooed as No. 2, but, in addition, with rows of dots and rings on back (pl. XII, 1).

Skin dry, muddy yellow brown.

Hair black. Hairs of head 65 cm. long (a record of length) falling over shoulders and back in ringlets. Slight moustache. Hair developed on extensor surface of upper and fore-arms, legs, and between shoulder blades, where there is profuse secretion of perspiration.

Height 152·4 cm.

Weight 108 lbs.

Cephalic length 19·3 cm.; breadth 13·6 cm.

Face. Wrinkles on forehead; superciliary ridges and glabella not marked. Eyebrows united across middle line by fine hairs. Cheek-bones rather prominent, with hollows beneath.

Nose straight. Height 4·1 cm.; breadth 3·5 cm. Ears not outstanding. Length 6·1 cm. Points well developed. Lobules attached, pierced. Possesses ear-rings, but will

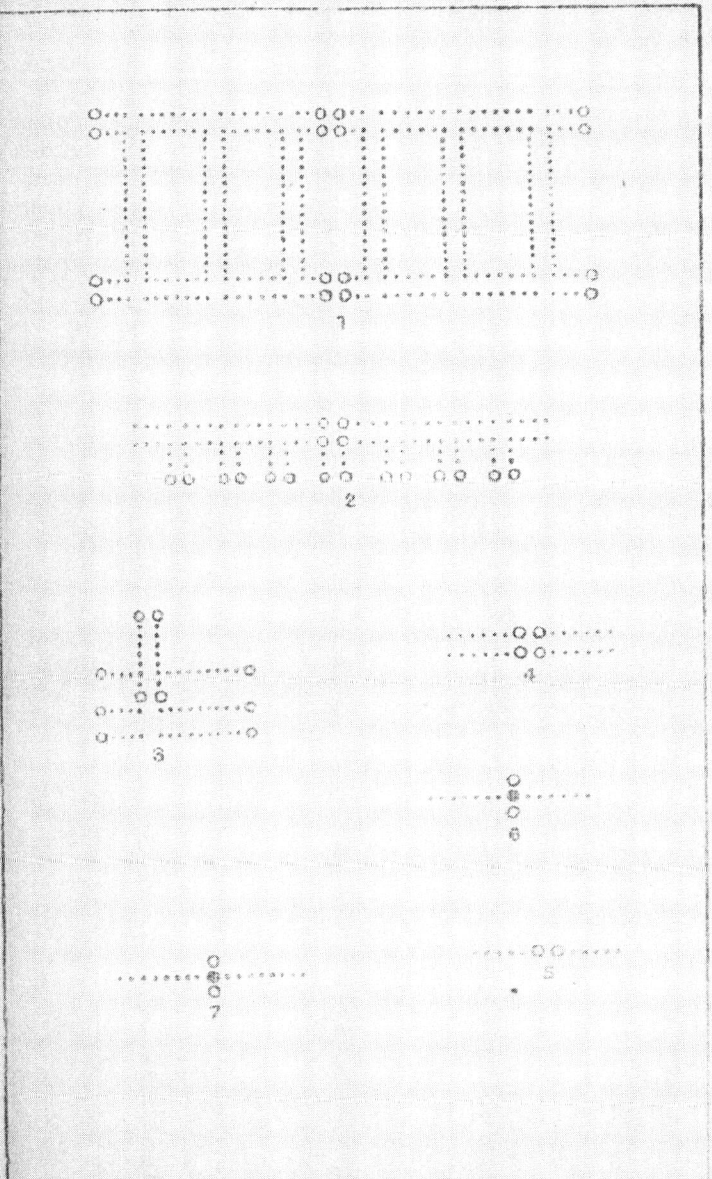

TODA TATTOO MARKS

PHOTO-ZINCO SURVEY OFFICE MADRAS
1895

not wear them until the dry funeral ceremony of an aunt, who died three months ago, has been performed.

Height from vertex to chin 21·5 cm. Bizygomatic breadth 12·2 cm. Bigoniac breadth 9·2 cm.

Shoulders 34·2 cm.

Hand, length 17·5 cm.; breadth 7·8 cm. Length of middle finger 11 cm. Nails of left hand kept long for combing and scratching.

Foot, length 24·7 cm.; max: breadth 7·9 cm.

13. Woman aged 35. Father a Kuttan; husband a Kenna. Five children (3 boys, 2 girls) all alive; youngest eight years old. Tattooed as No. 4. Linen bound round elbow-joint to prevent chafing of heavy brass armlets. Cicatrices of sores in front of elbow-joint produced by armlets.

Rudimentary whiskers and moustache, and long, straggling hairs on chin. Abundant development of hair on extensor surface of fore-arms.

Conjunctivæ injected. Long hairs directed upwards, uniting eyebrows across middle line. Ears pierced. Lobules not attached.

14. Woman, aged 23. Father a Kuttan; husband a Pekkan. One child (boy) three years old. Tattooed only below calves, and above ankles.

Nose concave. Height 4·1 cm.; breadth 3·1 cm. Broad throughout, and flat across bridge. Breadth between inner ends of eye-brows 2·5 cm.

Upper eyelid turns down at inner angle, so as to partially cover caruncle.

Broad lower jaw; bigoniac measuring 10 cm. (average= 9·4 cm).

15. Girl, aged 9–10. Hair in long curls (41 cm.), not shaved. Downy hairs on back, and extensor surface of fore-arm. Incipient moustache. Eye-brows united across middle line by long hairs directed upwards. Not reached puberty.

Height 134·6 cm.
Cephalic length 17·1 c.m.
,, breadth 13·3 c.m.
Bigoniac 9·1 c.m.
Bizygomatic 10·8 c.m.
Nasal height 3·6 c.m.
,, breadth 2·8 c.m.
Shoulders 28·7 c.m.
Span of arms 136·4 c.m.

Cubit 36·5 cm.
Hand, length 14·8 c.m.
,, breadth 6·1 c.m.
Middle finger 9·4 c.m.
Foot length 20·5 c.m.
,, breadth 5·9 c.m.

Dwelling places.

The odorous abode of the Todas is called a mand (village or hamlet) which is composed of huts, dairy temple, and cattle-pen, and has been so well described by Dr. Shortt, that I cannot do better than quote his account verbatim. "Each mand," he says, "usually comprises about five buildings or huts, three of which are used as dwellings, one as a dairy, and the other for sheltering the calves at night. These huts form a peculiar kind of oval pent-shaped construction, usually 10 feet high, 18 feet long, and 9 feet broad. The entrance or doorway measures 32 inches in height and 18 inches in width, and is not provided with any door or gate; but the entrance is closed by means of a solid slab or plank of wood from 4 to 6 inches thick, and of sufficient dimensions to entirely block up the entrance. This sliding door is inside the hut, and so arranged and fixed on two stout stakes buried in the earth, and standing to the height of 2½ to 3 feet, as to be easily moved to and fro. There are no other openings or outlets of any kind either for the escape of smoke or for the free ingress and egress of atmospheric air. The doorway itself is of such small dimensions that, to effect an entrance, one has to go down on all fours, and even then much wriggling is necessary before an entrance effected. The houses are neat in appearance, and are built of bamboos closely laid together, fastened with rattan, and covered with thatch which renders them water-tight. Each building has an end walling before and behind, composed of solid blocks of wood, and the sides are covered in by the pent-roofing which slopes down to the ground. The front wall or planking contains the entrance or doorway. The inside of a hut is from 8 to 15 feet square, and is sufficiently high in the middle to admit of a tall man moving about with comfort. On one side there is a raised platform or pial formed of clay, about 2 feet high, and covered with sambar (deer) or buffalo skins, or sometimes with a mat. This platform is used as a sleeping place. On the opposite side is a fire-place, and a slight elevation on which the cooking utensils are placed. In this part of the building faggots of firewood are seen piled up from floor to roof, and secured in their place by loops of rattan. Here also the rice-pounder or pestle is fixed. The mortar is formed by a hole dug in the ground, 7 to 9 inches deep, and hardened by constant use. The other household goods consist of 3 or 4 brass dishes or plates, several bamboo measures, and sometimes a hatchet. Each hut or dwelling is surrounded by an enclosure or wall formed of loose stones piled up 2 to 3 feet high, and includes a space or yard measuring 13 × 10 feet.

"The dairy, which is also the temple of the mand, is sometimes a building slightly larger than the others, and usually contains two compartments separated by a centre planking. One part of the dairy is a store-house for ghee, milk and curds, contained in separate vessels. The outer apartment forms the dwelling place of the pujāri or pālkārpāl (dairy priest). The doorways of the dairy are smaller than those of the dwelling huts, being 14 × 18 inches. The dairy or temple is usually situated at some little distance from the habitations, and strangers never attempt to approach too near it for fear of incurring the ill-will of the deity who is believed to preside within. Females are excluded, and the only parties who are free to come and go are the boys of the family. The flooring of the dairy is level, and at one end there is a fire place. Two or three milk pails or pots are all that it usually contains.

"The huts where the calves are kept are simple buildings somewhat like the dwelling huts.

"In the vicinity of the mands are the cattle-pens or tuels, which are circular enclosures surrounded by a loose stone wall with a single entrance guarded by powerful wooden stakes. In these the herds of buffaloes are kept at night. Each mand possesses a herd of these animals."

Sexual.

When a girl has reached the age of puberty, she goes through an initiatory ceremony, and a man of strong physique decides whether she is fit to enter into the married state. The selected man may subsequently marry the girl, or she may marry some one else, whom she accepts as meeting with her approbation. A man who is betrothed to a girl may enjoy conjugal rights before marriage with a view to testing mutual liking or dislike before it is too late, but may not live in the same hut with her.

No precautions are adopted to guard against pregnancy, and it is not viewed as a scandal if a girl becomes pregnant before marriage. If a man suspects his fiancéé of being pregnant by another, he may break off the engagement. The suspected man, if convicted, is not obliged to marry her.

It appears to be regarded as a mild disgrace if a child is born before marriage, but the girl is not banished from her mand.

If a married woman is found to be unfaithful to her husband, he may obtain a divorce, which is decreed by a panchāyat, or council, of Todas (a rudimentary type of judge and jury), and send her back to her parents. She is permitted to marry again, provided that her new husband makes good, in money or buffaloes, the expenses incurred in connection with the first marriage ceremony. In case of adultery, when punishment short of divorce is desired, a fine of a buffalo may be inflicted by the panchāyat, before whom the case comes up for hearing.

It is considered a disgrace for a woman not to get married, and, if she does not succeed in securing a husband by the natural process of sexual selection, her father bribes a man to marry her by a present of a buffalo. In ordinary marriages the bride's father receives a dowry of five rupees from the bridegroom-elect.

It is not looked on as a disgrace for a woman to be barren, but is attributed to bad luck, which may be remedied by prayers and propitiatory offerings to the swāmi. If satisfied that his wife is barren, a man may take unto himself a second wife, and live with both in one hut. Or his original wife may re-marry, if she can find a man ready to take her, provided that the expenses of her marriage with her first husband are refunded or made good, and jewelry returned.

When a woman is left a widow (barudi) she may live with her sons, if grown up and capable of supporting her, or with a married daughter, if her husband does not object to the constant presence of his mother-in-law. If she is left with young children, she returns to her parents. Widows are permitted to marry again. The name barudi, it may be noted, is applied to old women, widows, and barren women.

No test of virility or physical fitness is required of young men before entering into the married state, and no operation, *e.g.*, circumcision, is performed.

Girls are said to reach puberty between the ages of ten and twelve, and frequently 'join their husband' (to use the Toda phrase) about a year later.

TODA WOMAN.

During menstruation a woman lives apart in a separate hut. No purificatory ceremonies are performed.

When a woman discovers that she is pregnant with her first child, she removes the tāli (marriage badge) from her neck, and puts it aside until the ceremony in celebration of the fifth month of her pregnancy called *purs yet pimmi.* To witness this, Todas are invited to the mand, and feasted on rice, milk, and molasses (jaggery). The woman's father promises his son-in-law a buffalo by name, which is sent as a present subsequently. Husband and wife then go to the forest, accompanied by their relatives and guests, and the husband sets off in search of a blade of grass and twig of a shrub (*Sophora glauca*), while the woman remains seated at the foot of a nāga tree (*Eugenia Arnottiana*) near which a rude temporary hut has been erected. A triangular hole is cut in the tree a few feet above the ground, and a lighted lamp placed in the hole. The husband then asks his father-in-law, *purs pul godvayi*, 'Shall I tie the táli ?' and, on receiving assent to do so, places it round his wife's neck, and gives the grass and twig to her. After raising them to her head, the woman places them against the tree, under the lamp, and stands facing towards the tree until the lamp goes out. Meanwhile her husband ties up in a cloth some rāgi (*Eleusine Corocana*) wheat, honey, sāmai (*Panicum miliare*) and gram (*Cicer arietinum*), and places them in a round hole in the tree beneath the lamp. He then prepares a meal for himself and his wife, which they partake of separately towards evening. The other Todas return to the husband's mand, where they "dine and sleep," going on the following morning to the forest to bring back the man and his wife to the mand.

The twig and grass used in the above ceremony are made to represent a bow and arrow, and are, according to Mr. Natesa Sastri, placed in the niche along with the light, and the husband and wife observe it minutely for an hour. The bow and string in the form of a circle are afterwards tied round the neck of the woman, who is from this minute the recognised wife of the Toda who married her. The primitive marriage badge made from what the forest affords is retained only during that night. It is next morning replaced by a silver badge called kyavilli, between Rs. 30 and Rs. 50 in value.

" At any time before the birth of a child is expected, the husband or wife may sever their relationship from each other by a panchāyat or council of elders, and by returning the *put kudivan* with any presents that one party has received from another. Generally the presents do not take place till after a child is expected. When such an event seems certain, a ceremony called the *ur vot pimmi* takes place. This means the banishment from the house. On the first new moon day after this a spot is cleared out near the puzhar, in which rice with molasses is cooked in a new pot. An elderly woman rolls up a rag to the size of a small wick, dips it in oil, lights it up, and with the burning end scalds the woman's hands in four places—one dot at each of the lowest joints of the right and left thumbs, and one dot on each of the wrists. Then two stumps a foot high of the puvvu tree—(*Rhododendron arboreum*)—are prepared and rolled up in a black cumbly (a rough woollen cloth). These two stumps are called pirinbon and pirivon—he and she devils. Between these two a lamp is placed on the ground, and lighted. Two balls of rice cooked in the new pot near the puzhar are then brought, and placed before the pirinbon and pirivon on a kakonda leaf. The top of the balls are hollowed, and ghee is profusely poured into each while the following incantation is repeated :—pirinbon pirivon podya—may the he-devil and the she-devil eat this offering! This is something like the *bhūtabali* offered by the Hindus to propitiate the evil deities. After this offering the woman takes her food, and continues to live for one month in the puzhar till the next new moon, when she is again brought back to her own mand." (S.M. Natesa Sastri.)

A pregnant woman continues to live in the same hut as her husband until the time of delivery, and is then removed to a hut called puzhar, set apart for the purpose at a short distance from the mand, unless the mand possesses a boath (see p. 173), in which case the hut is situated at a distance of about two miles from the mand.

A woman skilled in the duties of a midwife from the same or some other mand tends the parturient woman. If the midwife is a near relative, no remuneration is awarded in return for her services; otherwise she receives board and lodging, and a present of a new putkūli. The woman's husband is not admitted into the hut during the time of delivery.

The woman is delivered on her hands and knees, or lying backwards, supported on her hands. Death during, or as a sequel of parturition, is said to be very rare. The umbilical cord is tied and cut.

If the child is born dead, or dies before it has taken the breast, it is buried. If, however, it has taken the breast, it is burned, and both green and dry ceremonies are performed.

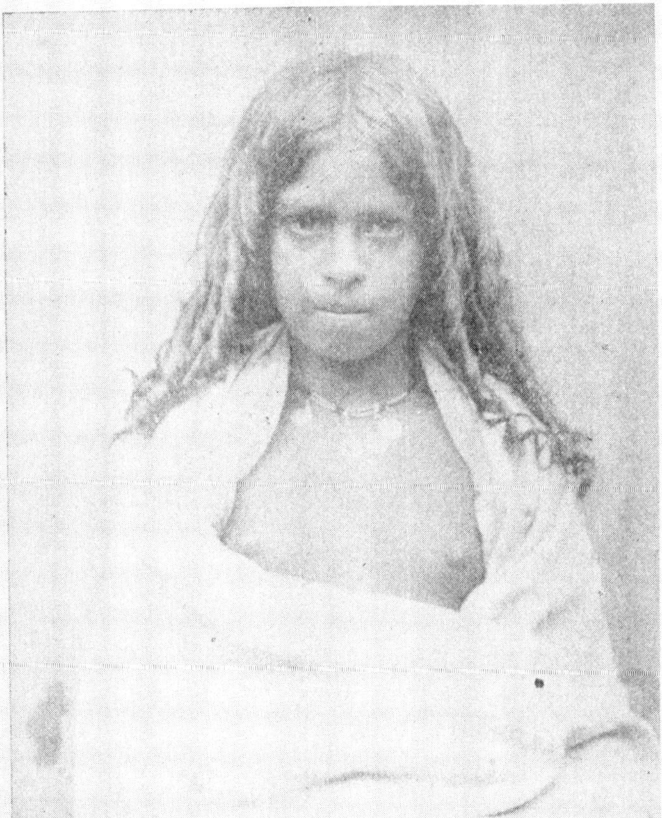

TODA GIRL.

On the day after delivery, or as soon after as possible, a young buffalo calf is brought in front of the puzhar, and the father of the new-born babe goes to the forest to make two new bamboo measures. The woman comes out of the hut with her infant, and sits at a distance of some yards from the calf. The husband on his return fills one, and half fills the other measure with water. Holding the measure which is half full on the right side of the calf's hind-quarters, he pours water from the measure which is full down the animal's back, so that some of it trickles into the other measure. A Toda, who has obtained from the jungle a leaf of the pālai tree (*Mappia fœtida*), places it in the hands of the woman. Her husband then pours water from one of the measures into the leaf, of which the woman drinks, and, if the child is a girl, puts a drop of water into its mouth. Man and wife, with the child, then return to the puzhar[7] where they live till the next new moon, when they return to their hut in the mand. A buffalo is then milked by a Toda belonging to the Pekkan clan. A leaf of the pālai tree is placed in the woman's hand, and milk is poured into it by a female relative, and drunk by the woman. In the evening a feast is given to the Todas who have been present at the returning home ceremony.

When the child has reached the third month of its existence,[8] it is, if a boy, taken by its father, unaccompanied by its mother, early in the morning to the dairy temple (pālchi) of the mand, before which the father prostrates himself, and offers up prayers to the swāmi. The child is named by a relative, *e.g.*, its maternal uncle or grand-father, after a relative, god, buffalo, mountain peak, &c., but in after life a nick name, sometimes indecent, is given. "They have," a friend writes to me, "curious nick names, these Todas. One little lad went by the name of 'Kacheri,' *i.e.*, public office. His elder brother, who was celebrated in the mand for his rendering of an interminable Badaga song, of which, one Ráman—a veritable Launcelot—was the hero, rejoiced in the title of 'Sirkar,' *i.e.*, Government." The simple baptism ceremony is followed by a feast, of which the inhabitants of the mand take part. If the child is a girl, it is not taken to the pālchi, but is merely named by its father.

---

[7] According to another version, the husband returns to his own hut, and does not live in the puzhar.

[8] Fortieth day according to another version.

The foregoing account of the *post partum* and naming ceremonies is recorded as it was narrated to me; but they are treated of more fully by Mr. Natesa Sastri, who no doubt had greater ease than a European in eliciting information, and from whose account the following extract is taken :—

"As soon as the child is born, the mother and baby are taken to a temporary hut (mand) built of sticks in a semi-circular form near a place in the general mand from which the Todas get their water-supply. A she-buffalo calf is brought before this hut, and the father of the child pours water on the left side of the calf between two sticks of the Nilgiri reed called odai, and the water is then collected in the hollow of a third reed stick. Then the mother and her new-born baby are made to sit in the temporary hut, and a leaf of kakonda tree (*Mappia fœtida*), is placed on their heads, and the collected water in the reed is poured on the leaf with the following incantation :—*Podur ner als pimi*—I pour the sacred water over you. This answers to the jatakarmam of the Hindu, which should be performed as soon as the child is born, though it is the custom now-a-days to reserve this to a latter date. After this the mother and baby retire to the puzhar, where they live till the next new moon. On the morning of the new moon day all the buffaloes in the mand are milked, and the collected milk is kept without being used by anybody. At twilight the same evening, after all the cattle have been penned, an elderly woman in the mand proceeds to the puzhar with a little milk in her hand in a vessel called nak (alak?) to bring the mother and baby to the father's house. A single leaf of the kakonda tree is given to the mother, which she holds in the form of a cup. The old woman pours into it three drops of milk. Each time a drop is poured, the mother raises the cup to her forehead, touches her hair with it, and drinks it off. Then the old woman conducts the mother and baby home, which is lighted up. From this moment the woman and the baby become members of the family. The Toda baby boy is wrapped up in a thick cotton cloth, called duppatti, and the face is never shown to any one. The mother feeds it till it is three months old. At the end of the third month a curious ceremony takes place called *mutarderd pimmi*, or opening the face ceremony, and it is as follows. Just before dawn on the third new moon day after the birth of the child, the father, who has not seen its face till then, takes it to the temple in the mand—the sacred dairy or pālchi—and worships at the door as follows :—

Vishzht tomma—May the child be all right!
Tann nimma—May God protect him!
Sembor kumma—May he give him life!

"After this prayer the father returns home with the child, and from this minute the wrapping up of the child's face ceases, and every one can look at it.

"If the maternal uncle of the child is present, another ceremony is also conjoined with *mutarderd pimmi.* It is the giving of a name to the boy allied to the *namakarana* of the Hindus.

"The ceremony of naming is called *tezhantu pimmi.* The uncle gives a name, and that is all. Then the ends of the hair of the baby are cut. A wild rose stick, called by the Toda kodag (*Rosa leschnaultiana*), is brought from the forest, the hair of the boy is placed on it, and with a sharp knife the edges that rest on the stick are cut off, and carefully preserved in a piece of cloth or paper tightly tied, and locked up in a box for three years. The reason for this, the Toda says, is that, if the bits are thrown away, and are used by the crows in building their nests, the head of the boy will never rest firm on his shoulders, but will always be shaky. After three years a deep pit is dug outside the limits of the mand, and the hair so carefully preserved is buried in it very carefully beyond the reach of the dreaded crow. When the boy is three years and three months old, the head is shaved, three locks of hair only being preserved. Two locks on the forehead are called meguti, and the third lock on the back of the head is called kut. This ceremony is called *kut mad vas pimmi.* All these rites are common to both male and female children born in a family. If the female child has an elder brother, she wears only the two front locks without the back one. If she is the first female child in the family—first in order of birth, or first surviving—she wears all the three locks."

Women are said to suckle their children from one to two years on an average.

There is no superstition in connection with the birth of twins, though one man, whom I questioned on the subject, was inclined to attribute the dual birth to the practice of polyandry; and I was reminded of the reply of a Ceylonese native to Professor Haeckel:—"These people have always had a number of fathers, and, as they inherit all the bad qualities of so many fathers, it is only natural that they should grow worse and worse."

In 'the Tribes inhabiting the Neilgherry hills,' 1856, by a German missionary, it is stated that "it is rarely that there are more than two or three children, and it is not at all an uncommon thing to find only a single child, while many families have none at all." Studied with reference to the above observation, which, it must be borne in mind, was written thirty-six years ago, the following statistics, gleaned in the course of my enquiries, are not without interest :—

Age of woman.	Male issue.	Female issue.	Remarks.
17	...	1	Seven months old.
25	2	1	Girl dead.
28	...	3	Two living, aged twelve and eight.
35	3	2	Youngest two years old. All living.
40	2	5	One male, two females, alive. Youngest aged twelve.
28	4	...	Two alive, aged six and a year and a half.
22	...	1	Nine months old.
30	1	4	All dead, except eldest girl aged twelve.
23	...	2	Both dead.
23	1	...	Three years old.
30	...	4	Youngest six years old. All living.
40	5	5	Only one alive, a female twenty-five years old (probably syphilitic).
30	1	1	Boy alive, six years old.
30	2	2	Youngest four years old. All living.
30	1	...	Eight months old.
35	3	2	Youngest eight years old. All living.
26	2	...	Youngest two years old. Both alive.
30	2	1	Youngest six years old. All living.
26	...	...	No issue.
28	...	...	
30	...	...	
	29 (20 living)	34 (19 living)	

PL. XV.

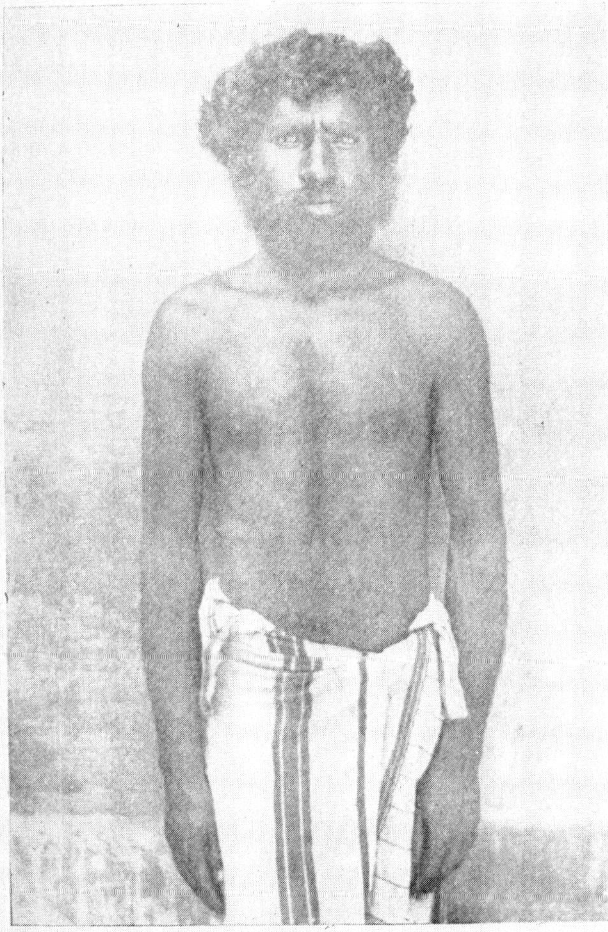

TODA MAN.

The Todas are endogamous as a tribe, and even as regards some of the five clans, viz., Kenna, Kuttan, Paiki, Pekkan and Todi, into which they are subdivided. Members of the different clans have no distinguishing dress or mark. Intermarriage between Paiki and Pekkan is said to be forbidden, but the remaining clans intermarry freely. Of twenty-seven cases examined by me, husband and wife belonged, as shown by the following tabular statement, to different clans in twenty-four, and to the same clan (Todi) in three cases only—figures which, as the cases were taken at random, demonstrate the prevalence of the custom of intermarriage between members of different clans :—

Intermarriage of clans.

Husband.	Wife.	Number of cases.
Kenna.	Todi.	7
Kenna.	Kuttan.	2
Kuttan.	Kenna.	2
Kuttan.	Todi.	1
Paiki.	Todi.	1
Pekkan.	Kuttan.	1
Pekkan.	Todi.	2
Todi.	Kenna.	4
Todi.	Kuttan.	3
Todi.	Pekkan.	1
Todi.	Todi.	3

Breeks states that " Todas are divided into two classes, which cannot intermarry, viz. :—

(1) Dêvalyâl.
(2) Tarserzhâl.

"The first class consists of the Peiki clan, corresponding in some respects to Brahmans; the second of the four remaining clans, the Pekkan, Kuttan, Kenna and Todi.

" The Peikis eat apart; and a Peiki woman may not go to a village of the Tarserzhâl, although the women of the latter may visit Peikis."

In the course of my enquiries, two different stories were told in connection with the marriage of Paikis, and the classes into which the Todas are divided. According to one story, Paikis may become either pālāls or kāltamāks (herdsmen of the tiriēri), and a Paiki who has a right to become a kāltamāk may marry into another clan, whereas a Paiki who has a right to become a pālāl may only marry into his own clan.

One girl I saw, a thirteen-year old bride of three months standing, belonging to the Todi clan, whose husband, a Paiki, had an hereditary right to become a kāltamāk. According to the other story, Todas are divided into two classes, Tērtāl and Tārtāl, of which the former comprises superior Paikis who may become pālāls or kāltamāks, and are only permitted to marry into their own clan; and the latter comprises Todis, Kennas, Kuttans, Pekkans, and inferior Paikis, who may marry into other clans, and cannot become either pālāls or kāltamāks. The man who gave me the latter version informed me further that, when a funeral ceremony is going on in the house of a Tērtāl, no Tārtāl is allowed to approach the mand; and that, when a Tērtāl woman visits her friends at a Tārtāl mand, she is not allowed to enter the mand, but must stop at a distance from it. Todas as a rule cook their rice in butter milk, but, when a Tērtāl woman pays a visit to a Tārtāl mand, rice is cooked for her in water. When a Tārtāl woman visits at a Tertāl mand, she is permitted to enter into the mand, and food is cooked for her in butter milk. Males of either class may enter freely into the mands of the other class. The restrictions which are imposed on Tērtāl women are said to be due to the fact that on one occasion a Tērtāl woman, on a visit at a Tārtāl mand, folded up a cloth, and placed it under her putkūli as if it was a baby. When food was served, she asked for some for the child, and, on receiving it, exhibited the cloth. The Tārtāls, not appreciating the mild joke, accordingly agreed to degrade all Tērtāl women.

Religion.

The religion of the Todas may be briefly summed up as being a simple faith handed down from generation to generation, adulterated, in modern times, with an admixture of Hinduism. They worship Kadavul, the creator of the earth and sky, to whom they pray night and morning that he will protect their cattle, their wives and families. They also worship the rising (but not the setting) sun, and the moon. They believe that the souls of the departed go, accompanied by the souls of the buffaloes killed at their funeral, to heaven (āmnād) over Makurti peak, and that one who has led a good life will there have enjoyment, and one who has led a bad life will suffer punishment. They believe, in a half-hearted manner, the story handed down from their ancestors that on the road to heaven there is a river full of leeches (familiar pests to them during the rainy season), which has to be crossed by a thread, which will break beneath the weight of a bad man and plunge him into hell (pūfērigēn),[9] but will carry a good man safely across. They believe further that a man who has led a bad life on earth returns thither in the guise of a giant or demon, who goes about killing Todas and other races. A good man is, in the Toda estimation, one who is given to deeds of charity, and a bad man one who is uncharitable (this in order of precedence), quarrelsome, thieving, &c.

One woman I saw, who was unable to come and have her measurements recorded, as she was pregnant, and could not cross the bridge which spanned the intervening Paikāra river; to cross the running water during pregnancy being forbidden by the swāmi (god) who presides over the river. Another woman wore round her neck a copper plate wound into a spiral, on which mantras were inscribed. She had suffered, she informed me, from evil dreams when laid up with fever, and wore the plate to keep away dreams and threatenings from devils.

The Todas reverence especially the hunting god Bētakan (who was the son of Dirkhish, who was the son of En, who was the first Toda), who has a temple—Bētakan swāmi kōvil—at Nambalakōd in the Wynād, and Hiriadēva, the bell-cow god, whose temple is at Mēlur, where Badagas perform the quaint and picturesque ceremony of walking through fire. They worship also the Hindu god Ranganātha at the temples at Nanjengōd in Mysore, and Karamaddi, near Mettupalaiyam, at the base of the hills, offering up cocoanuts, plantains, &c. If a woman is barren, the husband, with or without his wife, makes a pilgrimage to the temple, and prays to the swāmi to give them offspring. My informant, whose wife had born him no children, had gone to the temple at Nanjengōd about six months previously, and his wife was five months pregnant. The reputation of the shrine was consequently much enhanced, the woman's pregnancy being attributed to the intervention of the lingam (the phallic emblem).

A man who came to my laboratory had his hair hanging down in long tails reaching below his shoulders. He had, he told me, let it grow long, because, though married to him five years, his wife had presented him with no child. A child had, however, recently been born, and as soon as the dry funeral (kēdu) of a relation had been performed, he was going to sacrifice his locks as a thank-offering at the Nanjengōd shrine, where both Todas and Badagas worship.

---

[9] Pūf, leech; ēri, place; gen, water.

So far as I have been able to ascertain, the Todas have only one purely religious ceremonial, which takes the form of a buffalo sacrifice, and is called kona shastra. This ceremony is said to be performed once in four or five years,[10] with a view to propitiating the gods, so that they may bring good luck to the Todas, and make their buffaloes yield milk in abundance. A round hole is dug in the ground, and filled with salt and water, which is drunk by the grown up buffaloes and a selected buffalo belonging to the mand which is celebrating the rite. The Toda men (women are not permitted to take part in the ceremony) who have been invited to be present are then fed. The buffalo calf is killed by a priest (varzhāl or pālikarpāl), clad in a black putkūli round the waist, by a blow on the head with a stick made from a bough of the sacred *tūd* tree (*Meliosma pungens*). The assembled Todas then salute the dead animal by placing their foreheads on its head. The flesh, I was informed, is given to Kotas, but Breeks [11] states that "the flesh must not be boiled, but roasted on a fire, made by rubbing together two sticks of the neralu, muthu, or kem trees, and eaten by the celebrants."

Writing in 1872, Breeks remarked [12] that "about Ootacamund a few Todas have latterly begun to imitate the religious practices of their native neighbours. Occasionally children's foreheads are marked with the Sīva spot, and my particular friend Kinniaven, after an absence of some days, returned with a shaven head from a visit to the temple of Sīva at Nanjangudi." The following extracts from my notes will serve to illustrate the practice of marking (which seems to be done in some instances 'for beauty's sake,' and not from any religious motive) and shaving as carried out at the present day.

1. Man, aged 28. Has just performed a religious ceremony at the tiriēri (temple). White curved line painted across forehead, and dots below outer ends of curved line, glabella, and outside orbits (a common type of Badaga sect on mark). Smeared across chest, over outer side of upper arms and left nipple, across knuckles and lower end of left ulna, and on lobes of ears.

2. Man, aged 21. Painted on forehead as above. Smeared over chest and upper eye lids.

---

[10] According to Breeks (Primitive Tribes of the Nilagiris) an annual ceremony.

[11] *Op. cit.*

[12] *Op. cit.*

PL. XVI.

TODA MAN.

3. Man, aged 35. White spot painted on forehead.

4. Man, aged 30. Hair of head and beard cut short owing to death of grandfather.

5. Boy, aged 12. Shock-head of hair, cut very short all over owing to death of grandfather.

6. Girl, aged 8. Hair shaved on top, back and sides of head behind ears, and in median strip from vertex to forehead. Wavy curls hanging down back and side of neck.

7. Boy, aged 6. White spot painted between eyebrows. Hair shaved on top and sides of head, and in median strip from vertex to forehead. Hair brought forward in fringe over forehead on either side of median strip, and hanging down back of neck. [This boy's cephalic length was very large for his age, being the same as the average length of the adult Toda woman's head (18·4 cm.).]

8. Male child, aged 18 months. White spot painted between eyebrows. Shaved on top and sides of head. Hair brownish-black, wavy.

Priesthood.

The Toda priesthood includes five kinds of priests (dairymen), who rank as follows in order of precedence :—

(1) Pālāl (priests of the tiriēris).
(2) Vorzhāl.
(3) Kokvalikarpāl (at the Tārnāt mand).
(4) Kurpulikarpāl (at the Kāndal mand).
(5) Pālkarpāl (called Tarvēlikarpāl at the Tārnāt mand).

Pālāl and Tiriēri.—We visited a tiriēri (dairy temple or lactarium) at Paikāra by appointment, and on arrival near the holy spot, found the two pālāls (monks), well built men aged about thirty and fifty, respectively, clad in black cloths, and two kāltamāks (herdsmen)—youths aged about eight and ten—naked save for a langūti, seated on the ground, awaiting our arrival. As a mark of respect to the pālāls the three Todas who accompanied us arranged their putkūlis so that the right arm was laid bare, and one of them, who had assumed a turban in honour of his appointment as my guide, removed the offending head-gear. A long palaver ensued in consequence of the pālāls demanding ten rupees to cover the expenses of the purificatory ceremonies which, they maintained, would be necessary if I desecrated the tiriēri by photographing it. Eventually, however, under promise of a far smaller sum, the tiriēri was successfully photographed with pālāls, kāltamāks, and a domestic cat seated in front of it.

A typical tiriēri comprises a dwelling hut for the pālāls, a separate hut for the kāltamāks, a large and small cattle-pen (the latter for cow buffaloes in milk) for the sacred herd (swāmi mārdu), and tiriēri, or dairy temple, which contains the sacred bell (māni) and dairy appliances. No Todas, except pālāls and kāltamāks, are allowed within the tiriēri grounds.

The bell-cow is more sacred than the other members of the herd. On the decease of a bell-cow, the bell descends to her daughter, or, if she leaves no female offspring, a cow is brought from another tiriēri. The bell-cow does not usually wear the bell, but does so when a move is made to a distant tiriēri, for the periodical change of pasture-ground.

I interviewed a man, aged thirty-two, who had formerly been a pālāl for four years, but, getting tired of celibate existence, resigned his appointment so as to take a wife to himself. He had recently been to Nanjengōd to pray for a child to be given to him. His wife was pregnant, and his hair long, and hanging down below his shoulders. He told me that when the child was born, he would offer up thanks at the Nanjengōd shrine, have his hair cut, and give a meal to a hundred Badagas and others.

When a Toda is about to become a pālāl, he lives in the forest for two or three days and nights, naked except for a langūti, feeds on one meal of rice daily, and is allowed a fire to protect him from the cold night air. Many times during the two or three days he drinks, from a cup made of leaves, the juice of the bark of the tūd tree (*Meliosma pungens*) obtained by hitting the bark with a stone. On the last day of retreat puja is done to a black cloth—the distinguishing garb of a pālāl—which is carried by kāltamāks to the forest, and given to the novice, who spreads it on the ground, pours tūd juice on it, and utters mantras over it, and goes clad in it direct to the tiriēri.

Before becoming a pālāl, a man must obtain sanction to hold office from a pānchāyat of leading Todas, who decide on his fitness to enter on the sacred duties. During the absence of a pālāl, if married, from his wife, she may be supported by her husband's brother, or by her sons, or is placed under the charge of a man (not of necessity a relative) deputed by the pālāl, who defrays expenses, to take care of her, while he is off duty in his capacity as husband. A pālāl may resign office whenever he likes, on receipt of permission from a pānchāyat to do so; but eighteen years formerly, and ten to twelve years at the present day, are, I am told, the maximum time of service. On resigning, he returns to his mand, and is no longer regarded as a swāmi, descending abruptly from god-head to the routine life of a common Toda.

When a man or youth is about to become a kāltamāk, he retires for a day and night to the forest, naked save for a langūti, and on the following morning drinks some juice of the tūd tree, dons a white cloth, and is taken to the tiriēri. While within the precincts of the tīriēri, except in his own hut, he must go naked. No fixed time is allotted for service as a kāltamāk, and a kāltamāk may eventually become a pālāl.

The duties of a pālāl are as follows. Early in the morning he opens the cattle-pen, and sends the sacred herd out to graze, in the charge of the kāltamāk. After ablution, he enters within the tiriēri, and performs puja to the bell-god. About 7–30 or 8 A.M. he comes out of the tiriēri, ties a black cloth round his waist, and salutes the herd, which has returned from grazing, by raising his wand and bamboo measure (khāndi) to his head, and milks the cows. After milking, the buffaloes are again sent out to graze, and the milk is taken to the tiriēri, where further pujas are performed. On entering the tiriēri, the pālāl dips his fingers in milk three times, puts his fingers on the bell-god, and apparently utters the names of some gods, but my informant (an ex-pālāl) was hazy about their names. The morning meal is then cooked for both pālāl and kāltamāks. Every three or four days the pālāl makes butter and ney. Between 4 and 5 P.M. the buffaloes return home, and are penned for the night. Then follow more pujas, the evening meal, and retirement for the night.

On some days a pālāl may have to attend a pānchāyat at some distance from the tiriēri, whereat he acts as judge, enquiring into cases and delivering judgment, which is accepted by the other members of the pānchāyat. Or the members of the pānchāyat may assemble outside the precincts of the tiriēri, at some distance from the pālāl, but within range of hearing.

Milk, butter, and ney are purchased from the tiriēri by Todas and Badagas. The pālāl brings the buffalo produce outside the sacred precincts, keeping the intending purchasers at a distance, and, when he has returned to the triēri, the produce is removed, and its value in money left in its stead.

If there are more bulls than are required in the sacred herd, the surplus stock is given as a perquisite to the kāltamāks, and sold to Badagas or Todas. The flesh of dead members of the herd is given as a present to Kotas.

The following information relating to the priests of the Kāndal and Tārnāt mands was extracted with great difficulty.

At the Kāndal mand there are two dairy temples called kurpūli and orzhālli. The priests are called kurpūllikārpāl and vorzhāl. The former is a Kenna, paid six rupees per annum, and selected for office by the head-man of the mand. His duties are to graze and milk the buffaloes belonging to his temple, to make butter and ney, to distribute the produce among the inhabitants of the mand, and perform pujas in the temple. He is subject to the control of the head-man of the mand, and has to obey his orders to go to bazárs, villages, &c. The vorzhāl is also selected by the head-man of the mand, and must be a Paiki or Pekkan. He is paid six rupees per annum, and his duties are similar to those of the kurpūlikarpāl, but he may not go away from the mand to bazárs or villages. During the absence of the kurpūlikarpāl, he may milk the buffaloes of the kurpūli; but the kurpūlikārpal, being inferior in rank, is not allowed to milk the buffaloes of the orzhālli. Neither of the two priests is bound to remain in office for a fixed time, but may resign on being relieved by a successor. So long as they remain in office, they are bound to a life of celibacy, but a married man may hold office, provided that he keeps apart from his wife.

At the Tārnāt mand there are three dairy temples called kokvēli, tarvēli, and orzhālli. The priests attached to the temples are called, respectively, kokvēlikarpāl, tarvēlikarpāl, and vorzhāl. Each temple has its own buffaloes. The kokvēlikarpāl milks the buffaloes, and sells the produce apparently for his own benefit. He is only allowed to remain in office for three years and is succeeded by his brother; the office remaining, by hereditary right, in one family.

The tarvēlikarpāl and vorzhāl milk the buffaloes belonging to their respective temples, and distribute the produce among the inhabitants of the mand. The vorzhāl is paid six rupees per annum. All three priests have to perform pujas in their temples in addition to dairy duties.

PL. XVII.

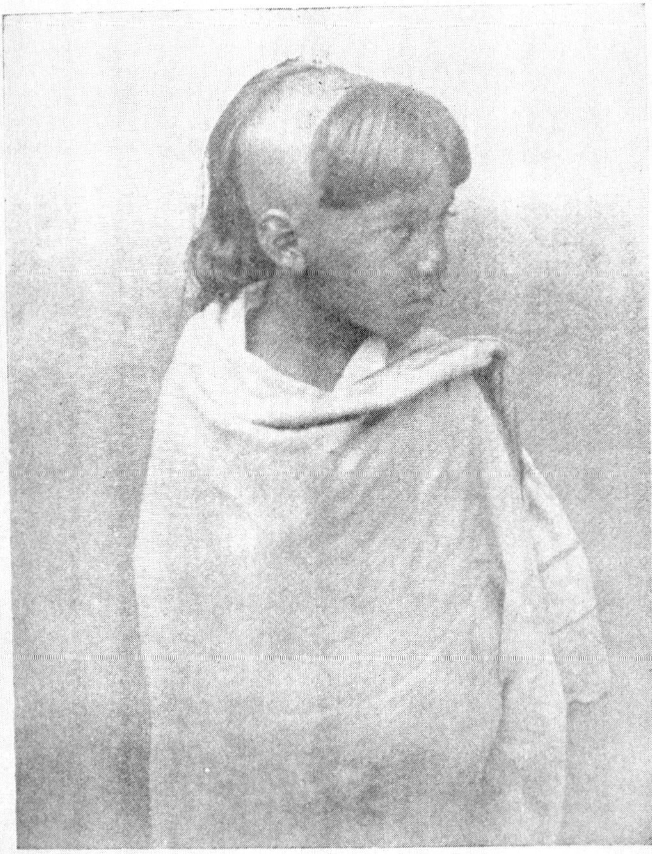

TODA BOY.

In addition to the pâlchis and tiriēris the Todas keep up as dairy-temples certain edifices called boaths or boas. Of these curious structures there are four on the Nilgiri plateau, viz., at the Muttanād mand, near Kotagiri, near Sholūr, and at Mudimand. The last was out of repair in 1894, but was, I was informed, going to be rebuilt shortly.

The Boath.

It has been suggested by Colonel Marshall [18] that the boath is not a true Toda building, but may be the bethel of some tribe contemporaneous with, and cognate to the Todas, which, taking refuge, like them, on these hills, died out in their presence ; and he compares them with the buildings, similar to the bothan or bee-hive houses in Scotland, which were discovered by the Rev. F. W. Holland in his explorations in the peninsula of Sinai.

The boath which we visited near the Muttanād mand, at the top of the Sigūr ghât, is known to members of the Ootacamund hunt as the Toda cathedral. It is a circular stone edifice, about 25 to 30 feet in height, with a thatched roof, and surrounded by a circular stone wall. The roof is crowned with a large flat stone. To penetrate within the sacred edifice was forbidden, but we were informed that it contains milking vessels, dairy apparatus, and a swāmi in the guise of a copper bell. Within the building no one is admitted except the pujāri (dairyman priest), who is called a vorzhāl. The present incumbent, who was out on the downs with the buffaloes at the time of our visit, was selected for office by the head-man of the village and his brother, and had been in office from ten to fifteen years.

In front of the cattle-pen of the neighbouring mand I noticed a grass covered mound, which, I was informed, is sacred. The mound contains nothing buried within it, but the bodies of the dead are placed near it, and earth from the mound placed on the corpse (dust to dust), which is then removed to the burning ground. At dry funerals the buffalo is slain near the mound.

Death ceremonies.

On the death of a Toda, the corpse, clad in a new putkūli and decorated with jewelry, in which the sick person has been dressed up when signs of approaching dissolution set in, is laid out in the hut. Marshall narrates the story that a man who had revived from what was thought his death-bed has been observed

[18] *Op. cit.*

parading about, very proud and distinguished looking; wearing the finery with which he had been bedecked for his own funeral, and which he would be permitted to carry till he really departed this life. A lamp is kept burning in the hut, and camphor used as a disinfectant. The news of the death are conveyed to other mands, the inhabitants of which join with the relatives of the departed one in weeping and mourning. Those who come to pay their respects to the dead body commence the customary signs of active grief when they have arrived within a short distance of the hut, on entering which they place their head to the head, and then their feet to the feet of the corpse, and mourn in company with the relatives. On the day of death, none of the inhabitants of the mand, or visitors from other mands, are allowed to eat food. On the following day meals, prepared by near relatives of the deceased, are served in another hut. The near relatives are forbidden to eat rice, milk, honey, or gram, until the funeral is over, but may eat rāgi, sāmai, butter, and ghī. If the head-man of a mand dies, the sons, and, if the head-woman dies, the daughters have, I was told, to observe the same rules as to diet until the dry funeral is performed.

When a man dies, a bow and arrow obtained from the Kotas, his walking stick, jaggery, rice, honey, cocoanuts, plantains, tobacco, a bamboo khāndi (measure), and cowries, with which to purchase food in the celestial bazár, are burned with him. Bags of rupees are, as a mere form, placed on the funeral pyre, but removed before the flames reach them.

When a woman dies, cooking and household utensils, jewelry, and articles of food, thread, and cowries are burned, and bags of rupees placed on the pyre.

The remains of gold and silver jewelry are recovered from the ashes, and made up again into jewelry.

Dry funeral.

It was my good fortune to have an opportunity of witnessing the dry funeral ceremony (kēdu) of a woman who had died from small-pox two months previously. On arrival at a mand, on the open downs about five miles from Ootacamund, we were conducted by a Toda friend to the margin of a dense shola,[14] (grove) where we found two groups seated apart, consisting of (a) women, girls, and brown-haired female babies, chat-

[14] Owing to the performance of rites in sacred groves it has been suggested that the Toda religion is Druidical or Celto-druidical.

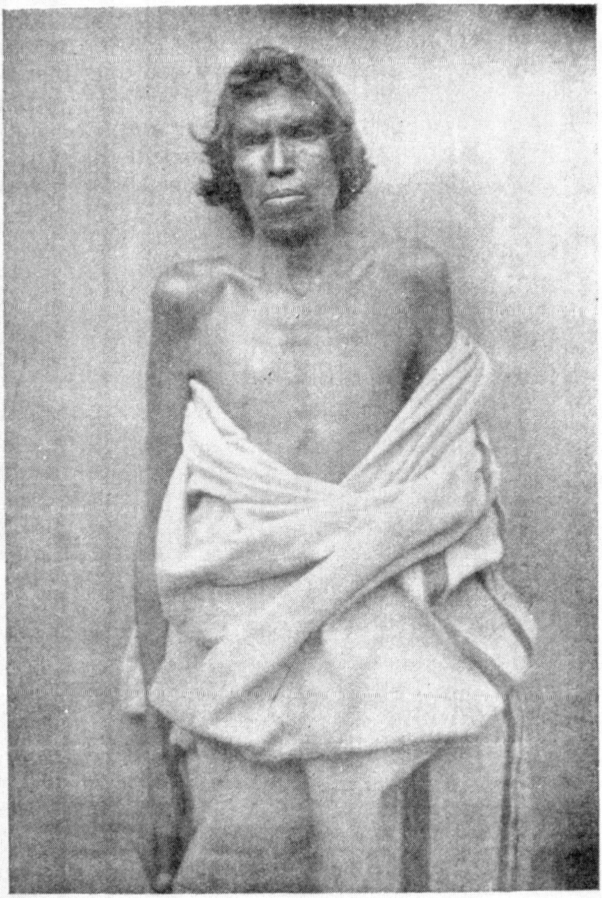

TODA MAN.

ting round a camp fire; (*b*) men, boys, and male babies carried, with marked signs of paternal affection, by their fathers. The warm copper hue of the little girls and young adults stood out in noticeable contrast to the dull, muddy complexion of the elder women.

In a few minutes a murmuring sound commenced in the centre of the female group. Working themselves up to the necessary pitch, some of the women (near relatives of the dead woman) commenced to cry freely, and the wailing and lachrymation gradually spread round the circle, until all, except little girls and babies who were too young to be affected, were weeping and moaning, some for fashion, others from genuine grief. The men meanwhile showed no signs of sorrow, but sat talking together, and expressed regret that we had not bought the hand dynamometer, to amuse them with trials of strength.

In carrying out the orthodox form of mourning, the women first had a good cry to themselves, and then, as their emotions became more intense, went round the circle, selecting partners with whom to share companionship in grief. Gradually the group resolved itself into couplets of mourners, each pair with their heads in close contact, and giving expression to their emotions in unison. Before separating, to select a new partner, each couple saluted by bowing the head and raising the feet of the other, covered by the putkūli, thereto.

From time to time the company of mourners was reinforced by late arrivals from distant mands, and, as each detachment, now of men, now of women, came in view across the open downs, one could not fail to be reminded of the gathering of the clans on some Highland moor. The resemblance was heightened by the distant sound as of pipers, produced by the Kota band (with two police constables in attendance), composed of four truculent-looking Kotas, who made a hideous noise with drums and flutes as they drew near the scene of action. The band, on arrival, took up a position close to the mourning women. As each detachment arrived, the women, recognising their relatives, came forward and saluted them in the manner customary among Todas by falling at their feet and placing first the right then the left foot on their head (ababuddiken).

Shortly after the arrival of the band, signals were exchanged, by waving of putkūlis, between the assembled throng and a small detachment of men some distance off. A general move was made, and an impromptu procession formed, with men in front, band in the middle, and women bringing up the rear. A halt was made opposite a narrow gap leading into the shola; men and women sat apart as before, and the band walked round, discoursing unsweet music. A party of girls went off to bring fire from the spot just vacated for use in the coming ceremonial, but recourse was finally had to a box of tändstikers lent by one of our party. At this stage of the proceedings we noticed a woman go up to the eldest son of the deceased, who was seated apart from the other men crying bitterly, and would not be comforted in spite of her efforts to console him.

On receipt of a summons from within the shola, the assembled Toda men and ourselves swarmed into it by a narrow track leading to a small clear space around a big tree, from a hole cut at the base of which an elderly Toda produced a piece of the skull of the dead woman, wrapped round with long tresses of her hair. It now became the men's turn to exhibit active signs of grief, and all with one accord commenced to weep and mourn. Amid the scene of lamentation, the hair was slowly unwrapt from off the skull, and burned in an iron ladle, from which a smell as of incense arose. A bamboo pot of ghī (clarified butter) was produced, with which the skull was reverently anointed, and placed in a cloth spread on the ground. To this relic of the deceased the throng of men, amid a scene of wild excitement, made obeisance by kneeling down before it, and touching it with their foreheads. The females were not permitted to witness this stage of the proceedings, with the exception of one or two near relatives of the departed one, who supported themselves sobbing against the tree.

The ceremonial concluded, the fragment of skull, wrapt in the cloth, was carried into the open, where, as men and boys had previously done, women and girls made obeisance to it.

A procession was then again formed, and marched on until a place was reached, where were two stone-walled kraals, large and small. Around the former the men, and within the latter the women, took up their position, the men engaging in chit-chat, and the women in mourning, which after a time ceased, and they too engaged in conversation, one of their number (a Toda beauty) entertaining the rest by exhibiting a photograph of herself, with which I had presented her.

A party of men, carrying the skull, still in the cloth, set out for a neighbouring shola, where a kēdu of several other dead Todas was being celebrated; and a long pause ensued, broken eventually by the arrival of the other funeral party, the men advancing in several lines, with arms linked, keeping step and crying out ā !, u !, ā !, u !, in regular time. This party brought with it pieces of the skulls of a woman and two men, which were placed, wrapt in cloths, on the ground, saluted, and mourned over by the assembled multitude. At this stage a small party of Kotas arrived, and took up their position on a neighbouring hill, waiting, vulture-like, for the carcase of the buffalo which was shortly to be slain.

Several young men now went off across the hill in search of buffaloes, and speedily re-appeared, driving five buffaloes before them with sticks. As soon as the beasts approached a swampy marsh at the foot of the hill, on which the expectant crowd of men was gathered together, two young men of athletic build, throwing off their putkūlis, made a rush down the hill, and tried to seize one of the buffaloes by the horns, with the result that one of them was promptly thrown. The buffalo escaping, one of the remaining four was quickly caught by the horns, and, with arms interlocked, the men brought it down on its knees, amid a general scuffle. In spite of marked objection and strenuous resistance on the part of the animal—a barren cow—it was, by means of sticks freely applied, slowly dragged up the hill, preceded by the Kota band, and with the 'third standard' student pulling at its tail. Arrived at the open space between the two kraals, the buffalo, by this time thoroughly exasperated, and with blood pouring from its nostrils, had a cloth put on its back, and was despatched by a blow on the poll with an axe deftly wielded by a young and muscular man (pl. xv). On this occasion no one was badly hurt by the sacrificial cow, though one man was seen washing his legs in the swamp after the preliminary struggle with the beast; but Colonel Ross-King narrates[15] how he saw a man receive a dangerous wound in the neck from a thrust of the horn, which ripped open a wide gash from the collar bone to the ear.

With the death of the buffalo, the last scene which terminated the strange rites commenced; men, women, and children pressing forward and jostling one another in their eagerness to salute the dead beast by placing their heads between its horns, and weeping and mourning in pairs; the

---

[15] Aboriginal Tribes of the Nilgiri Hills, 1870.

facial expression of grief being mimicked when tears refused to slow spontaneously.

A few days after the kēdu ceremony we were invited to be present at the green funeral of a girl, five years old, who had died of small-pox four days previously. We proceeded accordingly to the scene of the recent ceremony, and there, in company with a small gathering of Todas from the neighbouring mands (among them the only white-haired old woman whom I have seen), awaited the arrival of the funeral cortēge, the approach of which was announced by the advancing strains of Kota music. Slowly the procession came over the brow of the hill; the corpse, covered by a cloth, on a rude ladder-like bier, borne on the shoulders of four men, followed by two Kota musicians; the mother carried hidden within a sack; relatives and men carrying bags of rice and jaggery (molasses), and bundles of wood of the nāga tree (*Eugenia Arnottiana*) for the funeral pyre.

Green Funeral.

Arrived opposite a small hut, which had been specially built for the ceremonial, the corpse was removed from the bier, laid on the ground, face upwards, outside the hut, and saluted by men, women, and children, with same manifestations of grief as at the dry funeral. Soon the men moved away to a short distance, and engaged in quiet conversation, leaving the females to continue mourning round the corpse, interrupted from time to time by the arrival of detachments from distant mands, whose first duty was to salute the dead body. Meanwhile a near female relative of the dead child was busily engaged inside the hut, collecting together in a basket small measures of rice, jaggery, sago, honey-comb, and the girl's simple toys, which were subsequently to be burned with the corpse.

The mourning ceasing after a time, the corpse was placed inside the hut, and followed by the near relatives, who there continued to weep over it. A detachment of men and boys, who had set out in search of the buffaloes which were to be sacrificed, now returned driving before them three cows, which escaped from their pursuers to re-join the main herd. A long pause ensued, and, after a very prolonged drive, three more cows were guided into a swampy marsh, where one of them was caught by the horns as at the kēdu ceremony, and dragged reluctantly, but with little show of fight, to the weird strains of Kota drum and flute,

TODA MAN.

in front of the hut, where it was promptly despatched by a blow on the poll.

The corpse was now brought from within the hut, and placed, face upwards, with its feet resting on the forehead of the buffalo, whose neck was decorated with a silver chain, such as is worn by Todas round the loins to suspend the langūti, as no bell was available, and the horns were smeared with butter. Then followed the same frantic manifestations of grief as at the kēdu, amid which the unhappy mother fainted from sheer exhaustion.

Mourning over, the corpse was made to go through a form of ceremony, resembling that which is performed at the fifth month of pregnancy with the first child. A small boy, three years old, was selected from among the relatives of the dead girl, and taken by his father in search of a certain grass and a twig of a shrub (*Sophora glauca*), which were brought to the spot where the corpse was lying. The mother of the dead child then withdrew one of its hands from the putkūli, and the boy placed the grass and twig in the hand, and limes, plantains, rice, jaggery, honey-comb, and butter in the pocket of the putkūli, which was then stitched with needle and thread in a circular pattern. The boy's father then took off his son's putkūli, and covered him with it from head to foot. Thus covered, the boy remained outside the hut till the morning of the morrow, watched through the night by near relatives of himself and his dead bride.

[On the occasion of the funeral of an unmarried lad, a girl is, in like manner selected, covered with her putkūli from head to foot, and a metal vessel, filled with jaggery, rice, etc. (to be subsequently burnt on the funeral pyre), placed for a short time within the folds of the putkūli. Thus covered, the girl remains till next morning, watched through the dreary hours of the night by relatives. The same ceremony is performed over the corpse of a married woman, who has not borne children, the husband acting as such for the last time, in the vain hope that the woman may produce issue in heaven.]

The quaint ceremonial concluded, the corpse was borne away to the burning-ground within the shola, and, after removal of some of the hair by the mother of the newly wedded boy, burned, with face turned upwards,[16] amid

[16] Marshall states that he was "careful to ascertain that the placing the body with its *face downwards* had not been an accidental circumstance."

the music of the Kota band, the groans of the assembled crowd squatting on the ground, and the genuine grief of the nearest relatives.

The burning concluded, a portion of the skull was removed from the ashes, and handed over to the recently made mother-in-law of the dead girl, and wrapped up with the hair in the bark of the tūd tree.

A second buffalo, which, properly speaking, should have been slain before the corpse was burnt, was then sacrificed, and rice and jaggery were distributed among the crowd, which dispersed, leaving behind the youthful widower and his custodians, who, after daybreak, partook of a meal of rice, and returned to their mands; the boy's mother taking with her the skull and hair to her mand, where it would remain until the celebration of the dry funeral.

No attention is paid to the ashes after cremation, but they are left to be scattered by the winds.

Games.

At the Muttanād mand we were treated to an exhibition of the games in which adult males indulge.

In one of these, called narthpimi, a flat slab of stone is supported horizontally on two other slabs fixed perpendicularly in the ground so as to form a narrow tunnel, through which a man can just manage to squeeze his body with difficulty. Two men take part in the game, one stationing himself at a distance of about thirty yards, the other about sixty yards from the tunnel. The front man, throwing off his cloth, runs as hard as he can to the tunnel, pursued by the 'scratch' man, whose object is to touch the other man's feet before he has wriggled himself through the tunnel.

Another game, which we witnessed, consists of trials of strength with a very heavy stone, the object being to raise it up to the shoulder; but a strong, well-built man—he who was entrusted with slaying the buffalo at the kēdu—failed to raise it higher than the pit of his stomach, though straining his muscles in the attempt. An old man assured us that, when young and lusty, he was able to accomplish the feat.

A still further game (ilāta) corresponds to the English tip-cat, which is epidemic at a certain season in the London bye-streets. It is played with a bat like a broom-stick, and a cylindrical piece of wood pointed at both ends. This piece of wood is propped up against a stone, and struck with the bat. As it flies up off the stone, it is hit to a distance with the bat, and caught (or missed) by the out-fields. At this game my Toda guide was very expert.

Breeks mentions that the Todas play a game resembling 'puss in the corner' and called kāriālapimi, which was not included in the programme of sports got up for our benefit.

We gave a demonstration of 'putting the stone,' and, if some future anthropologist finds this to be one of the Toda athletic sports, he must attribute its introduction to direct British influence.

Medicinal.

I was informed that, in former times, certain men among the Todas were credited with the power to cast out devils by treatment with herbs, and that devils are still cast out of Todas who are possessed with them by certain Badaga and Hindu exorcists. The Todas treat mild cases of sickness with herbs, and a red stone purchased in the Ootacamund bazár; but serious cases are treated at the Ootacamund hospital.

The Todas scornfully deny the use of aphrodisiacs, but both men and women admit that they take sālep misri boiled in milk 'to make them strong.' It is stated in the 'Pharmacographia Indica' (1893) that the "sālep of Madras is largely supplied from the Nilgiris, where it is collected by the Todas and other hill tribes." The district forest officer of the Nilgiris writes, however, more recently that there is now little or no trade, as the digging up of the roots has been prohibited in the reserve forests.

Sālep misri, it may be mentioned, is made from the tubers (testicles de chien) of various species of Eulophia and Orchis, belonging to the natural order Orchideæ.

Relations with other tribes.

When a Toda meets a Badaga he bends down, and the Badaga, as a form of greeting and sign of superiority, places his hand on the top of the Toda's head. The Todas believe that their tribe has always dwelt on the Nilgiris, and that the other tribes came up from the plains. When the Badagas arrived on the hills, they put under cultivation land which previously belonged to the Todas (who claim to have originally owned the whole of the Nilgiris). As 'compensation allowance,' the Badagas give grain of various kinds (*gudu*) to the Todas in proportion to the abundance of the crop, only objecting, it is said, to do so when the crop is short. But there is reason to believe that the Badaga is not inclined to give as freely at the present day as in times gone by, and the Toda is commencing to be thrown on his own resources as a means of gaining the equivalent of his daily bread.

Some years ago a Toda was found dead, in a sitting posture, on the top of a hill near a Badaga village, to which a party of Todas had gone to collect the tribute. The body was burned, and a report then made to the police that the man had been murdered. On enquiry it was ascertained that the dead man was supposed to have bewitched a little Badaga girl, who died in consequence; and the presumption was that he had been murdered by the Badagas out of revenge.

When a Toda meets a Kota, the latter kneels and raises the feet of the Toda to his head. From the Kotas the Todas acquire their iron implements (axes, māmutis, knives, &c.) and earthenware utensils. No payment in money is made, but, when a buffalo dies, the Kotas, who are eaters of carrion, are rewarded with the flesh, hide and horns. The Kotas supply the band at Toda tamāshas, *e.g.*, green and dry funerals; the musicians being paid in buffaloes and rice.

When a Toda meets a Kurumbar, the latter bends forward, and the Toda places his hand on the Kurumbar's head. The Todas and Kurumbars are not on good terms, and the Todas are afraid of them, because they are believed to be sorcerers, and to possess the power of casting the evil eye on them, and making them fall sick or die. My Toda guide—a stalwart representative of his tribe—expressed fear of walking alone from Ootacamund to Kotagiri, a distance of eighteen miles along a good road, lest he should come to grief at the hands of Kurumbars; but this was, as the sequel showed, a frivolous excuse to get out of accompanying me to a distance from his domestic hearth. The Kurumbars, when they come up to the plateau to get grain from the Badagas, apparently levy black mail on the Todas, and, if they demand money or buffaloes, the Todas dare not refuse to disgorge.

A Toda meeting an Irula is saluted in the same way as by a Kurumbar; but, so far as I can gather, there is but little communication between the Todas and Irulas.

Tenure of land.

The tenure under which lands are held by the Todas is summed up as follows by Mr. R. S. Benson in his report on the revenue settlement of the Nilgiris, 1885. "The earliest settlers, and notably Mr. Sullivan, strongly advocated the claim of the Todas to the absolute proprietary right to the plateau; but another school, led by Mr. Lushington, as strongly combated these views, and apparently regarded the Todas as merely occupiers under the ryotwari system in force

PL. XX.

TODA MAND.

generally in the presidency. From the earliest times the Todas have received from the cultivating Badagas an offering, or tribute, called '*gudu*,' or basket of grain, partly in compensation for the land taken up by the latter for cultivation, and so rendered unfit for grazing purposes, but chiefly as an offering to secure the favour, or avert the displeasure, of the Todas, who, like the Kurumbas, are believed by the Badagas, to have necromantic powers over their healths and that of their herds. The European settlers also bought land in Ootacamund from them, and to this day the Government pays them the sum of Rs. 150 per annum, as compensation for interference with the enjoyment of their pastoral rights in and about Ootacamund. Their position was, however, always a matter of dispute, until it was finally laid down in the despatch of the Court of Directors, dated 21st January, 1843. It was then decided that the Todas possessed nothing more than a prescriptive right to enjoy the privilege of pasturing their herds, on payment of a small tax, on the State lands. The Court desired that they should be secured from interference by settlers in the enjoyment of their munds (or village sites), and of their spots appropriated to religious rights. Accordingly pattas were issued, granting to each mand three bullahs (11·46 acres) of land. In 1863 Mr. Grant obtained permission to make a fresh allotment of nine bullahs (34·38 acres) to each mund on the express condition that the land should be used for pasturage only, and that no right to sell the land or the wood on it should be thereby conveyed. It may be added that the so-called Toda lands are now regarded as the inalienable common property of the Toda community, and unauthorized alienation is checked by the imposition of a penal rate of assessment (G.O., 18th April, 1882). Up to the date of this order, however, alienations by sale or lease were of frequent occurrence. It remains to be seen whether the present orders and subordinate staff will be more adequate than those that went before to check the practices referred to."

With the view of protecting the Toda lands, Government took up the management of these lands in 1893, and framed rules under the Forest Act for their management, the rights of the Todas over them being in no way affected by the rules, of which the following is an abstract :—

1. No person shall fell, girdle, mark, lop, uproot, or burn or strip off the bark or leaves from, or otherwise damage any tree growing on the said lands, or remove the timber,

or collect the natural produce of such trees or lands, or quarry or collect stone, lime, gravel, earth or manure upon such lands, or break up such lands for cultivation, or erect buildings of any description or cattle kraals; and no person or persons, other than the Todas named in the patta concerned, shall graze cattle, sheep, or goats upon such lands, unless he is authorised so to do by the Collector of the Nilgiris, or some person empowered by him.

2. The Collector may select any of the said lands to be placed under special fire protection.

3. No person shall hunt, beat for game, or shoot in such lands without a license from the Collector.

4. No person shall at any time set nets, traps, or snares for game on such lands.

5. All Todas in the Nilgiri district shall, in respect of their own patta lands, be exempt from the operation of the above rules, and shall be at liberty to graze their own buffaloes, to remove fuel and grass for their domestic requirements, and to collect honey or wax upon such lands. They shall likewise be entitled to, and shall receive free permits for building or repairing their munds and temples.

6. The Collector shall have power to issue annual permits for the cultivation of grass land only in Toda pattas by Todas themselves, free of charge, or otherwise as Government may, from time to time, direct; but no Toda shall be at liberty to permit any person, except a Toda, to cultivate, or assist in the cultivation, of such lands.

KOTA MAN.

II.—THE KOTAS OF THE NILGIRIS.

ACCORDING to Dr. Oppert "it seems probable that the Todas and Kotas lived near each other before the settlement of the latter on the Nīlagiri. Their dialects betray a great resemblance. According to a tradition of theirs (the Kotas), they lived formerly on Kollimallai, a mountain in Mysore. It is wrong to connect the name of the Kotas with cow slaying, and to derive it from the Sanskrit gōhatyā (cow-killer). The derivation of the term Kota is, as clearly indicated, from the Gauda-Dravidian word ko (ku), mountain, and the Kotas belong to the Gaudian branch."

The Kotas were returned at the census of 1891 as numbering 1,201 (556 males and 645 females) against 1,062 (498 males and 564 females) in 1881. They inhabit seven villages, of which six—Kotagiri (or Peranganād), Ḳīl-Kotagiri, Todanād, Mekanād, Kundanād, and Sholur—are situated on the plateau, and one is at Gudalur in the Wynād, on the northern slopes of the Nīlgiris. They form large communities, and each village consists of thirty to sixty or more detached huts and rows of huts arranged in streets. The huts are built of mud, brick, or stone, roofed with thatch or tiles, and divided into living and sleeping apartments. The floor is raised above the ground, and there is a verandah in front with a seat on each side, whereon the Kota loves to take his siesta, and smoke his cheroot in the shade, or sleep off the effects of a drinking bout. The door-posts of some of the huts are ornamented with carving executed by wood carvers in the plains. A few of the huts and one of the forges at Kotagiri have stone pillars sculptured with fishes, lotuses, and floral embellishments by stone carvers from the plains.

The Kotas have no caste, but are divided into kēris or streets, viz., kīlkēri, mēlkēri, and nadukēri. People belonging to the same kēri may not intermarry, as they are supposed to belong to the same family, and intermarriage would be distasteful. The following examples of marriage between members of different kēris were recorded in my notes :—

Husband.	*Wife.*
Kīlkēri.	Nadukēri.
Do.	Do.
Do.	Mēlkēri.
Nadukēri.	Do.
Mēlkēri.	Nadukēri.
Nadukēri.	First wife Kīlkēri, second wife Mēlkēri.

On the day following my arrival at Kotagiri on the eastern extremity of the Nīlgiri plateau, a deputation of Kotas from the neighbouring village waited on me, and, having learnt that I was a Government official, consented to allow me to record their measurements only on the distinct understanding that I would not get their land-assessment increased—a point on which they were unnecessarily suspicious of me. For a few days all went well; measurements were taken, and photographs duly admired. But the Kotas did not, like the Todas, enter good-humouredly into the spirit of an anthropological inquiry. A sudden strike set in, and an order was circulated among the village community that the measurement of women was not to be continued. The crisis was, however, after much argument and many interviews with leading representatives of the tribe, headed by an overfed monegar (head-man), who receives a small salary from Government to collect rent and make returns of vital statistics, overcome by the intervention of the local Tahsildar (revenue officer). As a sign that peace was declared, three ancient and shrivelled female hags turned up at the bungalow to be measured. Subsequently, however, yet another strike ensued, and I was unblushingly informed that all the women were *enceinte* and could not leave the village, though I met troops of them on the road every evening.

My first interview with the object of extracting information as to Kota 'manners and customs' (to use a time-honoured phrase) was not a conspicuous success; the man who was engaged to act as my informant arriving in a state of maudling intoxication, and dressed up in the cast-off clothes of a British soldier. However, an excellent substitute was found in an intelligent and well-to-do blacksmith, who, in return for a print of his photograph, cheroots, a new cloth, and money wherewith to purchase drink, became a faithful ally. To the pencil of this man is due the drawing of an elephant reproduced on plate XXII for comparison

TODA AND KOTA DRAWINGS

with the more crude efforts of a Toda lad to depict a man, a buffalo, and an elephant.

The besetting vice of the Kotas is a partiality for drink, and they congregate towards evening in the arrack shop and beer tavern in the bazár, whence they stagger or are helped home in a state of noisy and turbulent intoxication.

The Kotas are universally looked down on as being unclean feeders and eaters of carrion; a custom which is to them no more filthy than is that of eating game when it is high, or using the same tooth-brush day after day to a European. An unappetising sight, which may frequently be witnessed on roads leading to a Kota village, is that of a Kota carrying the flesh of a dead buffalo, often in a high state of putridity, slung on a stick across his shoulders, with the entrails trailing on the ground, so that "the very scent of the carrion—faugh—reached my nostrils at the distance where we stood." Colonel Ross King narrates[17] how he once saw a Kota carrying home for food a dead rat thrown out of the stable a day or two previously. When I repeated this story to my informant, he glared at me, and bluntly remarked (in Tamil) "The book tells lies." Despite its unpleasant nature, the carrion diet evidently agrees with the Kotas, who are a hard, sturdy set of men, flourishing, it is said, most exceedingly when the hill-cattle are dying of epidemic disease, and the food-supply is consequently abundant.

Though all classes look down on the Kotas, all are agreed that they are excellent artisans, whose services as blacksmiths, carpenters, rope and umbrella makers, etc., are indispensable to the other hill tribes. In fact the Todas believe that the Kotas are a caste of artisans specially brought up from the plains to work for them. Each Toda, Irula, Kurumba, and Badaga settlement has its Muttu Kotas, who work for the inhabitants thereof, and supply them with sundry articles called muttu in return for the carcases of buffaloes and cattle, ney (clarified butter), grain, and plantains. The Kotas eat the flesh of the buffaloes and cattle which they receive, and sell the horns to Labbi (Muhamadan) merchants from the plains. Chucklers (boot-makers) from the plains collect the bones (which the Kotas might utilise as a source of income), and purchase the hides, which are roughly cured by the Kotas with chunám

---

[17] *Op. cit.*

(lime) and ávaram bark (*Cassia auriculata*), and fastened to the ground with pegs to dry.

The Kota blacksmiths, who are skilled workmen, make hatchets, bill-hooks, knives, and other implements for the various hill tribes, especially the Badagas, and at times for 'Hindus' and Europeans. Within the memory of men still living they used to work with iron-ore brought up from the plains, but now depend on scrap-iron which they purchase locally in the bazár. The most flourishing smithy in the Kotagiri village is made of brick, of local manufacture, roofed with zinc, and fitted with appliances (anvil, pincers, &c.), of European manufacture.

As agriculturists the Kotas are said to be quite on a par with the Badagas, and they raise on the land adjacent to their villages extensive crops of potatoes, bearded wheat, kīrai (amaranth), sāmai (*Panicum miliare*), korāli (*Setaria italica*), mustard, onions, &c.

At the revenue settlement, 1885, the Kotas were treated in the same way as the Badagas and other tribes of the Nīlgiris, except the Todas, and the lands in their occupation were assigned to them at rates varying from 10 to 2 annas per acre. The 'bhurty' or shifting system of cultivation, under which the Kotas held their lands, was formally, but nominally, abolished in 1862–64; but it was practically and finally done away with at the revenue settlement of the Nīlgiri plateau. The Kota lands are now held on puttas under the ordinary ryotwari tenure.

In former days opium of good quality was cultivated by the Badagas, from whom the Kotas got poppy-heads, which their herbalist practitioners used for medicinal purposes. Now-a-days, however, the Kotas purchase opium in the bazár, and use it as an intoxicant.

The Kota women have none of the fearlessness and friendliness of the Toda, and, on the approach of a European to their domain, bolt out of sight, like frighted rabbits in a warren, and hide within the inmost recesses of their huts. As a rule they are clad in filthily dirty cloths, all tattered and torn, and frequently not reaching nearly as low as the knees. In addition to domestic duties, the women have to do work in the fields, fetch water, and collect fire-wood, with loads of which, supported on the head by a pad of bracken fern leaves, and bill-hook slung on the shoulder, old and young women, girls and boys, may continually be seen returning to the village. The women also make baskets, and rude earthen pots on a

KOTA WOMAN.

potter's wheel. This consists of a disc made of dried mud, with an iron spike, by means of which it is made to revolve in a socket in a stone fixed in the ground in the space in front of the houses, which also acts as a winnowing floor.

Education, in its most elementary form, cannot be said to have taken a keen grip of the Kotas; for, though a night-school has been established in their village at Kotagiri by the Basel Mission for the last eight years, at the time of my visit to Kotagiri only nine males, of various ages from twelve to twenty-four, out of a community of several hundreds, were on the school books.

Characteristics.

The chief characteristics of the Kotas, their personal ornaments, system of tattooing, &c., will be gathered from the following illustrative cases.

As a type of a Kota man the following case may be cited :—

No. 1. Male, aged 25. Name Komuttan. Blacksmith and carpenter. Silver bangle on right wrist; two silver rings on right little finger; silver ring on each first toe. Gold ear-rings. Langūti tied to silver chain round loins.

Height 164·4 cm.

Weight 125 lbs.

Skin of exposed parts rather darker than protected parts. (Unexposed parts, especially the chest, are in some Kotas markedly pale by contrast.)

Hair of head black, wavy, parted in middle, and tied in a bunch behind. Imperial moustache, waxed. Beard trimmed short. Hair well developed on chest, abdomen, extensor surface of forearms, and legs. Hair of axillæ shaved, as being an eye-sore. (The Kotas are not nearly such a hairy race as the Todas, but, as in Europeans, Brāhmans, etc., individuals are frequently met with, in whom the hairy system is well developed on the trunk and extremities.)

Forehead narrow and prominent. Countenance indicates decision of character. Length from vertex to chin 21·1 cm. Bizygomatic 12·7. Bigoniac 9·6 cm. Glabella and superciliary ridges not marked. Eyebrows bushy, united across middle line by thick hairs. Cheek-bones rather prominent. Lips thin. Facial angle (of Cuvier) 70°. Teeth white, and well formed. (The teeth of the Kotas are often discoloured from the habit of chewing betel.)

Eyes horizontal. Iris dark-brown.

Nose straight, narrow. Height 4·6 cm.; breadth 3·2 cm. Alæ expanded.

Ears not outstanding, shallow. Height 5·6 cm. Lobules not attached, pierced.

Cephalic length 19·1 cm.; breadth 14·2 cm.

Chest 83 cm. circumference.

Shoulders 38 cm.

Biceps 28·5 cm. circumference.

Cubit 45·6 cm.

Hand, length, 18·5 cm.; breadth 8·4 cm.

Thigh 45 cm. circumference.

Calf 32 cm. circumference.

Foot, length, 25·8 cm.; max: breadth 8·9 cm.

The average height of the Kota man, according to my measurements, is 162·9 cm.; but the following is an example of the tallest Kota whom I saw, and who considerably exceeds the mean.

No. 2. Male, aged 35. Carpenter. Light blue eyes inherited from his mother. His children have eyes of the same colour. Lobules of ears pendulous from heavy gold ear-rings set with pearls. Black hair on head and beard. Black, mixed with brown hairs, beneath lower lip, and in moustache. Nose aquiline. (Another Kota man with light blue eyes was also noticed by me.)

	Man No. 2.	Kota average.
Weight	130 lbs.	115 lbs.
Height	178·3 cm.	162·9 cm.
Do. sitting	90·4 „	85·8 „
Do. kneeling	121·4 „	120 „
Do. to gladiolus	131·6 „	120·6 „
Span of arms	190·2 „	168·3 „
Chest	86 „	83·3 „
Shoulders	40 „	37·7 „
Cubit	49·5 „	45·1 „
Hand, length	19·6 „	18 „
Do. breadth	8·7 „	8 „
Hips	28·5 „	27 „
Foot, length	26·7 „	25·2 „
Do. breadth	9·7 „	8·8 „

No. 3. Male. An old man, bearing a certificate from the Duke of Buckingham appointing him head-man of the Kota at Kotagiri, in recognition of his services and good character.

KOTA NAUTCH PARTY.

Says that he is sixty-five years old, but looks, and must be, many years older, as he appears as an elderly white-haired man in a photograph taken by Mr. Breeks more than twenty years ago. Bowed with age, and walks with support of a stick. (The Kotas, unlike the Todas, do not as a rule carry walking-sticks.) Bald over frontal and temporal regions. White hair on head and face, and long white hairs in middle of chest.

No. 4. Boy, aged 13. Height 145·4 cm. Shock head of hair, which is being permitted to grow where it was till recently shaved. Long tuft of hair hanging down from vertex below neck behind. Incipient moustache. Hair developed in axillæ, not on trunk. Bushy eyebrows united by dense hairs. Iris light brown. Silver bangle on right wrist; two silver rings on left first finger.

No. 5. Boy, aged 10–12. Hair shaved on top, sides, and back of head, leaving a tuft of long hair hanging down from vertex behind *á la* Hindu. Ears pierced. Forehead very prominent and narrow. Cephalic length 18·5 cm.; breadth 13·9 cm.

No. 6. Man. Hair tied behind in a bunch by means of a string with a silver ring attached to it.

No. 7. Man. Two letters of his name tattooed (blue) on front of left forearm.

No. 8. Man. Initial letter of his name tattooed (blue) on front of left forearm.

No. 9. Man. Branded with cicatrix of burn made, when a young man, with a burning cloth, across lower end of back of forearm. This is a distinguishing mark of the Kotas, and is made on boys when they are more than eight years old.

No. 10. Man. 'Grog-blossom' nose. Breadth of nose 4·6 cm. He is a confirmed drunkard, but attributes the inordinate size of his nasal organ to the acrid juice of a tree which he was felling dropping on to it.

No. 11. Woman, aged 30. Divorced for being a confirmed opium-eater, and living with her father. Dull, muddy complexion. Vacant expression of countenance. Skin of chest pale by contrast with the neck. Hair of head smooth, parted in middle, and done up behind in bunch round pad of leaves. Bushy eyebrows united across middle line by hairs. Slight moustache. Wears a dirty cotton cloth with blue and red stripes, covering body and reaching below knees, and a plain cotton loin-cloth. Two brass and glass bead necklets. Four copper rings on left upper arm above elbow. Two copper bangles separated by cloth ring on right wrist; two brass bangles separated by similar ring on left wrist. Brass ring on first toe of each foot. Blue tattooed line uniting eyebrows. Name in Tamil tattooed on right forearm. Two vertical tattooed lines on left upper arm. Tattooed with rings and lines on outer side of right upper arm (pl. XXVI, 1).

Height 146·6 cm.

Weight 86 lbs.

Shoulders 33·8 cm.

Cubit 40·9 cm.

Hand, length, 16·5 cm.; breadth 7·1 cm. Nails kept long for combing hair.

Foot, length, 22 cm.; max: breadth 7·7 cm.

Cephalic length, 18·2 cm.

,, breadth, 13·7 cm.

Forehead prominent. Bigoniac 9·4 cm. Bizygomatic 12·4 cm. Facial angle 68°. Teeth white and regular.

Nose, snub. Height 4·1 cm.; breadth 3·3 cm.

Ears pierced. Too poor to afford ear-rings.

12. Woman, aged 40. Two plain glass-bead necklets, and bead necklet ornamented with silver rings. Four brass rings and one steel ring on left forearm. Two massive brass bangles, weighing two pounds each, and separated by cloth ring, on right wrist. Brass bangle with brass and steel pendents, and shell bangle on left wrist. Two steel and one copper ring on right ring finger; brass rings on left first, ring, and little fingers. Two brass rings on first toe of each foot. Tattooed line uniting eyebrows. Tattooed on outer side of both upper arms with rings, dots, and lines (pl. XXVI, 2); rows of dots on back of right forearm; circle on back of each wrist; rows of dots on left ankle.

13. Woman, aged 35. Tattoo marks on forearms (pl. XXVI, 3 and 4).

14. Woman, aged 35. Tattoo marks on right upper arm (pl. XXVI, 5).

15. Woman, aged 25. Tattoo marks on right upper arm (pl. XXVI, 6) and left forearm (pl. XXVI,7).

16. Woman, aged 25. Tattoo marks on right upper arm (pl. XXVI, 8) and left forearm (pl. XXVI, 9).

17. Woman, aged 35. Glass necklet ornamented with cowry shells, and charm pendent from it, consisting of a

KOTA WOMEN.

fragment of the root of some tree rolled up in a ball of cloth. She put it on when her baby was about a month old, to protect it against devils. The baby has a similar kind of charm round the neck.

18. Woman, aged 30. Has been treated in hospital for syphilitic ulceration of the palate. History of primary syphilis.

Religion.

The Kota priesthood is represented by dēvādis and pūjāris, who wear no distinguishing dress. The office of dēvādi is carried on by heredity, and the pūjāris are appointed by the dēvādi when under the influence of inspiration by the swāmi (god). The dēvādi becomes at times possessed by the god, to whom he repeats the requests and desires of the people, and delivers to them the answer of the god. He is permitted to live with his wife, and not bound, like the Toda pālāl, to a celibate existence. On the death of a dēvādi, the god takes possession of some member of his family, who dreams that the mantle of the dead priest has descended on him, and becomes seized with inspiration in the temple.

In addition to the dēvādi, each village has two pūjāris, appointed by the dēvādi when under the influence of inspiration by the god. Their main duty is to perform pujas in the temple.

They too may be married, and live with their wives; but, at the great festival in honour of Kāmatarāya, neither dēvādi nor pūjāri may live or hold communion with their wives for fear of pollution, and they have to cook their meals themselves.

"Some rude image of wood or stone, a rock or tree in a secluded locality, frequently form the Kota's object of worship, and to which sacrificial offerings are made; but the recognised place of worship in each village consists of a large square piece of ground, walled round with loose stones, three feet high, and containing in its centre two[18] pent-shaped sheds of thatch, open before and behind, and on the posts (of stone) that support them some rude circles and other figures are drawn. No image of any sort is visible here" (Shortt). These sheds, which are a short distance apart, are dedicated to Siva and his consort Pārvati under the names of Kāmatarāya and Kālikai. Though

[18] At Kolamalé there are three temples, two dedicated to Kāmatarāya and one to Kālikai.

no representation of the swāmis is exhibited in the temples at ordinary times, their spirits are believed to pervade the buildings, and at the annual ceremony they are represented by two thin, plain plates of silver, which are attached to the upright posts of the temples. The stones surrounding the temples at Kotagiri are scratched with various quaint devices, and lines for the games of hulikotē and kotē.

The Kota villagers go, I was told, to the temple once a month, at full moon, and meditate on and worship god. Their belief is that Kāmatarāya created the Kotas, Todas, and Kurumbas, but not the Irulas. "Tradition says of Kāmatarāya that, perspiring profusely, he wiped from his forehead three drops of perspiration, and out of them formed the three most ancient of the hill tribes—the Todas, Kurumbas and Kotas. The Todas were told to live principally upon milk, the Kurumbas were permitted to eat the flesh of buffalo calves, and the Kotas were allowed perfect liberty in the choice of food, being informed that they might eat carrion if they could get nothing better." (Breeks.)

In comparatively recent years the Kotas have created a new god, named Māgāli, to whose influence outbreaks of cholera are supposed to be due; and a goddess, named Māriammā, is supposed by the Kotas to be responsible for small-pox. When cholera breaks out among the Kota community, special sacrifices are performed with a view to propitiating the wrath of the god. Māgāli is represented by an upright stone in a rude temple at a little distance from Kotagiri, where an annual ceremony is held, at which some man will become possessed, and announce to the people that Māgāli has come. At this ceremony a special priest (pūjāri) offers up plantains and cocoanuts, and makes a sacrifice of sheep and fowls. My informant, despite the fact that he was the pūjāri of Māgāli, was, or pretended to be, ignorant of the following legend recorded by Breeks as to the origin of the worship of the god of small-pox. "A virulent disease carried off a number of Kotas of Perangaṇāda, and the village was abandoned by the survivors. A Badaga named Munda Jogi, who was bringing his tools to the Kotagiri to be sharpened, saw near a tree something in the form of a tiger, which spoke to him, and told him to summon the run-away Kotas. He obeyed, whereupon the tiger form addressed the Kotas in an unknown tongue, and vanished. For some time the purport of this communication remained a mystery. At last, however, a Kota came forward to interpret, and declared that the god ordered the Kotas to return to the village on pain of a recurrence of the pestilence. The command was obeyed, and a swāmi house was built on the spot where the form appeared to the Badaga (who doubtless felt keenly the inconvenience of having no Kotas at hand to sharpen his tools)."

Sexual.

In a Report by Lieutenant Evans, written in 1820, it is stated that "the marriages of this caste (the Kothewars) remind one of what is called bundling in Wales. The bride and bridegroom being together for the night, in the morning the bride is questioned by her relatives whether she is pleased with her husband elect. If she answers in the affirmative, it is a marriage; if not, the bridegroom is immediately discharged, and the lady does not suffer in reputation if she thus discards half a dozen suitors." The recital of this account, translated into Tamil, raised a smile on the face of my Kota informant, who volunteered the following information relating to the betrothal and marriages ceremonies of the present day.

Girls, as a rule, marry when they are from twelve to sixteen years old, between which years they reach the age of puberty. A wife is selected for a lad by his parents, subject to the consent of the girl's parents; or, if a lad has no near relatives, the selection is made for him by the villagers. Betrothal takes place when the girl is quite a child (eight to ten). The boy goes, accompanied by his father and mother, to the house where the girl lives, prostrates himself at the feet of her parents, and, if he is accepted, presents his future father-in-law with a four-anna piece, which is understood to represent a larger sum. According to Breeks the boy also makes a present of a bīrianhana of gold, and the betrothal ceremony is called bali-med-deni (bali, bracelet; med-deni, I have made). Both betrothal and marriage ceremonies take place on Tuesday, Wednesday, or Friday, which are regarded as auspicious days.

The ceremonial in connection with marriage is of a very simple nature. The bridegroom elect, accompanied by his relatives, attends a feast at the house of his bride, and the wedding day is fixed. On the appointed day the bridegroom pays a dowry, varying from ten to fifty rupees, to his bride's father, and takes the girl to his house, where the wedding guests, who have accompanied them, are feasted.

The Kotas seem to be prolific, and families of eight, nine, ten or more are not uncommon; but it is rarely that the whole of a large family grows up, many dying in infancy. Widow remarriage is permitted.

The Kotas, as a rule, have only one wife, and polyandry is unknown among them. But in some instances polygamy is practised. My informant, for example, had two wives, of whom the first had only presented him with one child, a daughter; and, as he was anxious to have a son, he had taken to himself a second wife. If a woman bears no children, her husband may marry a second, or even a third wife; and, if they can get on together without fighting, all the wives may live under the same roof; otherwise they occupy separate huts.

Divorce may, I was told, be obtained for incompatibility of temper, drunkenness, or immorality; or a man can get rid of his wife 'if she is of no use to him,' *i.e.*, if she does not feed him well, or assist him in the cultivation of his land. Divorce is decided by a pānchāyat (council) of representative villagers, and judgment given, after hearing the evidence, by an elderly member of the community. Cases of theft, assault, or other mild offence are also settled by a pānchāyat, and, in the event of a case arising which cannot be settled by members of council representing a single village, delegates from all the seven villages meet together. If even then a decision cannot be arrived at, recourse is had to the official court, of which the Kotas steer clear if possible. At a big pānchāyat the head-man (pittakār) of the Kotas gives the decision, referring, if necessary, to some 'sensible member' of the council for a second opinion.

When a married woman is known to be pregnant with her first child, her husband allows the hair of the head and face to grow long, and leaves the nails of both hands uncut. At the time of delivery the woman is removed to a hut (a permanent structure) called vollūgūdi (vollū inside, gūdi nest), which is divided into two rooms, one of which serves as a lying-in hospital, the other for women at the menstrual periods. Women are attended in child-birth by a professional Kota midwife, who is remunerated with board and a new cloth. After the birth of the child the woman apparently remains in the vollūgūdi till the next full moon, and then goes for a further space of two months to another hut called tēlulu. On departure from the vollūgūdi the baby is fed with rice boiled, in a specially made clay pot, on a fire made with the wood of a particular jungle tree. When the woman leaves the tēlulu, a feast is given to the relatives, and the head-man of the khēri gives the child a name which has been

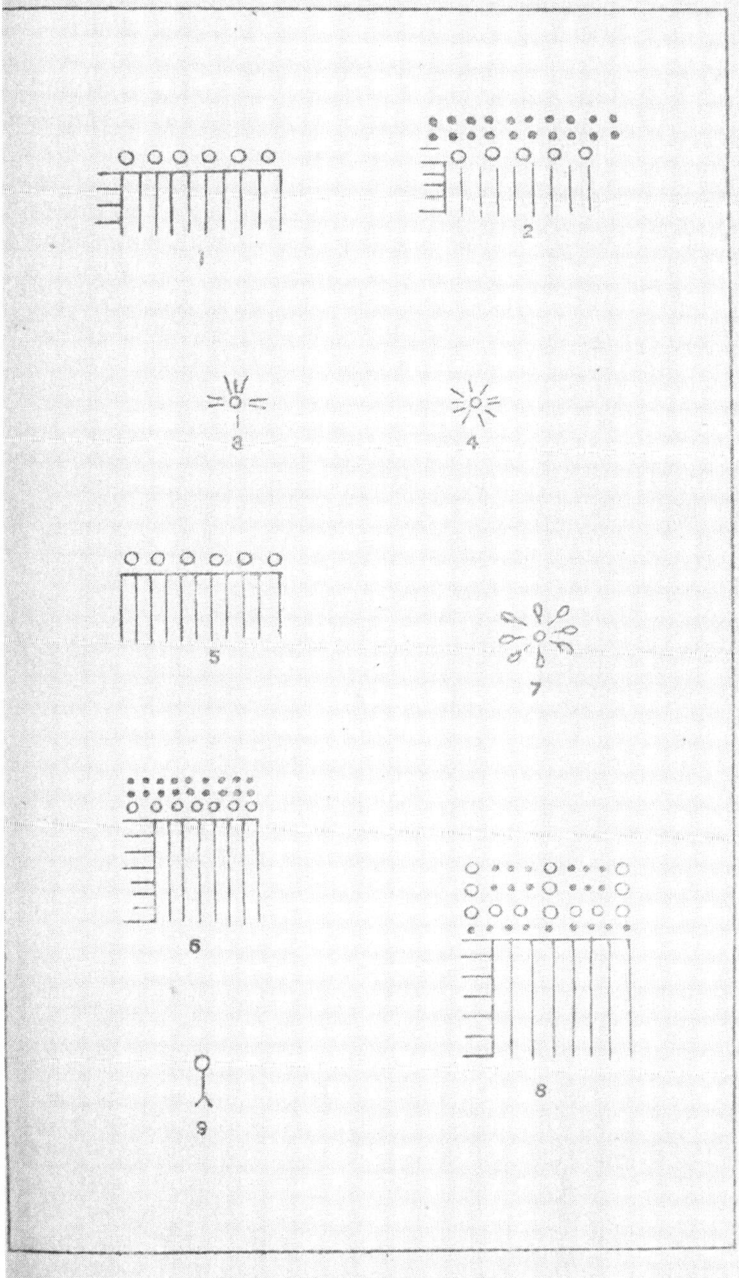

KOTA TATTOO MARKS

chosen by its father. Before the woman returns to her home, at the end of her temporary banishment therefrom, it is purified with cow-dung and water, and, as she enters her house, the man who has named the child gives her a few drops of water to drink. Breeks mentions that a woman with her first child, on leaving the vollūgūdi for the tēlulu, must make seven steps backwards among seven kinds of thorns strewed on the ground; but my informant expressed ignorance of any such ceremony.

A common name for females is Mādi, one of the names of the goddess Kālikai; and the first male child is always called Komuttan (= Kāmatarāya). The numerous Komuttans in a village are distinguished by the prefix big, little, carpenter, etc.

Funeral ceremony.

When a man or woman is on the point of death, a gold coin (virāya fanam) is placed in the mouth. After death the corpse is laid out on a mat, covered with a cloth, the thumbs are tied together with string, and the hands placed on the chest. The relatives of the deceased, the pūjāri and dēvādi, and Kotas of other villages who have been informed of the death, come and salute the corpse, head to head, and mourn over it.

A rude catafalque (tēru), made of wood and decorated with cloths, is placed in front of the house of the deceased, round which the Kotas dance to the strains of a Kota band, while the near relatives continue mourning. A male buffalo is fetched from a Badaga village or Toda mand, and killed outside the village, as at a Toda kēdu, from which some of the Kota funeral rites are borrowed. The carcase is skinned, cut up, and taken to the house where the corpse is lying. Half the flesh is distributed among the Kota villagers.

When the time of the funeral has arrived, the dead body is removed from the house, placed on a stretcher, and taken outside the village, with the catafalque borne in front, to a tree in the jungle. A cow (not buffalo) is then killed, the hand of the corpse placed on one of the horns, and all present salute it with the same ceremonial as at a Toda green funeral. The dead cow is handed over to pariahs, and not eaten by Kotas. From the jungle the corpse and catafalque are carried to the burning ground, where a funeral pyre is made, on which the corpse is laid face upwards, and burned beneath the catafalque. If the corpse be that of a man, jewelry, cheroots, various kinds of grain, iron implements, walking-stick, and buguri (musical instrument);

and, if of a woman, jewelry, a winnowing basket, rice measure, rice beater, sickle, cakes and rice are burnt. The widow of a dead man is said to place on the dead body her tāli (marriage badge) and other ornaments, which are, however, removed before the pyre is kindled.

On the day following that of the funeral, the smouldering ashes are extinguished with water, and the ashes, excepting the remains of the skull, collected together and buried in a pit, the site of which is marked by a heap of stones. The skull is buried separately in a spot which is also marked by a heap of stones. A feast, whereat the half of the buffalo which was not given to the villagers is served up as funeral baked meat, is then held.

In the month of December a dry funeral ceremony takes place, in imitation of the Toda bara kēdu. Eight days before the date fixed for the ceremony, a dance takes place in front of the houses of the Kotas whose memorial rites are to be celebrated, and three days before their celebration invitations are issued to the different Kota villages. On the appointed day the relatives of the deceased have buffaloes ready, and place the skulls, which have been unburied, wrapt in cloths, on a cot. Obeisance is made to the relics by touching them with the head. They are then carried to a shola (the funeral ground), where the buffaloes—one for each skull—decorated with a bell hung round the neck, are killed. The skulls are then burned with the same articles as at the burning of the corpse, with, in the case of a male, the addition of a pole (tarzh), twenty feet long, decorated with cowries, such as is burned at Toda dry funerals. The burning concluded, water is poured from a chatty over the ashes, on which no further care is bestowed. Those who have been present at the ceremony remain all night on the spot, where, on the following morning, a feast and dance take place. Finally a dance is held in the village; the dancers being dressed up as at the annual feast.

It may be noted that if a child only a few days old dies, the body is buried instead of being burnt.

Annual ceremony.

A great annual festival is held in honour of Kāmatarāya with the ostensible object of propitiating him with a view to his giving the Kotas an abundant harvest and general prosperity. The feast commences on the first Monday after the January new moon, and lasts for about a fortnight, which is observed as a general holiday, and is said to be a continuous scene of licentiousness and debauchery, much indecent dancing taking place between men and women. According to Metz, the chief men among the Badagas must attend the festival; otherwise their absence would be regarded as a breach of friendship and etiquette, and the Kotas would immediately avenge themselves by refusing to make any ploughs or earthen vessels for the Badagas.

The programme of events, so far as I have been able to gather without being present as an eye-witness, is somewhat as follows :—

First day.

A fire is kindled by one of the priests in the temple, and carried to the Nadukēri section of the village, where it is kept burning throughout the festival. Around the fire men, women, adolescent boys and girls, dance to the weird music of the Kota band, whose instruments consist of clarionet, drum, tambourine, brass horn, and buguri (Toda flute).

Second day
Third day
Fourth day
Fifth day
} Dance at night.

Sixth day.

The villagers go to the jungle, and collect bamboos and rattans, with which to re-roof the temples. Dance at night.

Seventh day.

The day is busily spent in re-roofing and decorating the temples, and it is said to be essential that the work should be concluded before night-fall. Dance at night.

Eighth day.

In the morning the villagers go to Badaga villages, and cadge for presents of grain and ghī which they subsequently cook, place in front of the temple as an offering to the swāmi, and, after the priests have eaten, partake of, seated round the temple.

Ninth day.

Kotas, Todas, Badagas, Kurumbas, Irulas and 'Hindus' come to the Kota village, where an elaborate nautch is performed, in which men are the principal actors, dressed up in gaudy attire consisting of skirt, petticoat, trousers, turban and scarves, and freely decorated with jewelry which is either their own property or borrowed from Badagas for the occasion. Women merely dressed in clean cloths, also take part in a dance called kumi, which consists of a walk round to time beaten with the hands. I was present at a private performance of the male nautch, which was as dreary as such entertainments usually are, but it lacked the go which is doubtless put into it when it is performed under natural conditions in the village away from the restraining influence of the European. The nautch is apparently repeated daily until the conclusion of the festival.

Eleventh and twelfth days.

A burlesque representation of a Toda kēdu (funeral ceremony) is given, at which the part of the sacrificial buffaloes is played by men with buffalo horns fixed on the head, and body covered with a black cloth.

At the close of the festival the pūjāris, dēvādi, and leading Kotas go out hunting with bows and arrows, leaving the village at 1 A.M. and returning at 3 A.M. They are said to have shot bison [19] at this nocturnal expedition; but what takes place at the present day is said to be unknown to the villagers, who are forbidden to leave their houses during the absence of the hunting party. On their return to the village, a fire is lighted with a hand fire drill by friction, a twig of the baiga tree, with cloth wrapped round its point, being twisted round in a socket in a plank until it ignites. Into the fire a piece of iron is put by the dēvādi, made red-hot with the assistance of the bellows, and hammered by the pūjāri. The priests then offer up a parting prayer to the swāmi, and the festival is at an end.

Games.

Like the Todas, the Kotas indulge in trials of strength with heavy spherical stones, which they raise, or attempt to raise, from the ground to the shoulders, and in a game resembling the English tip-cat. In another game sides are chosen, of about ten on each side. One side takes shots with a ball made of cloth at a brick propped up against a wall, near which the other side stands. Each man is allowed three shots at the brick. If the brick is hit and falls over, one of the 'outside' picks up the ball, and throws it at the other side, who run away and try to avoid being hit. If the ball touches one of them, the side is put out, and the other side go in.

A game, called hulikote, which bears a resemblance to the English child's game of fox and geese, is played on a stone chiselled with lines which forms a rude playing board. In one form of the game (pl. XXVII) two tigers and twenty-five bulls, and in another form (pl. XXVII) three tigers and fifteen bulls engage, and the object is for the tigers to take, or, as the Kotas express it, kill all the bulls. In a further game, called kotē, a labyrinthiform pattern, or maze, is chiselled on a stone, to get to the centre of which is the problem.

---

[19] *Bos gaurus*, the bison of European sportsmen.

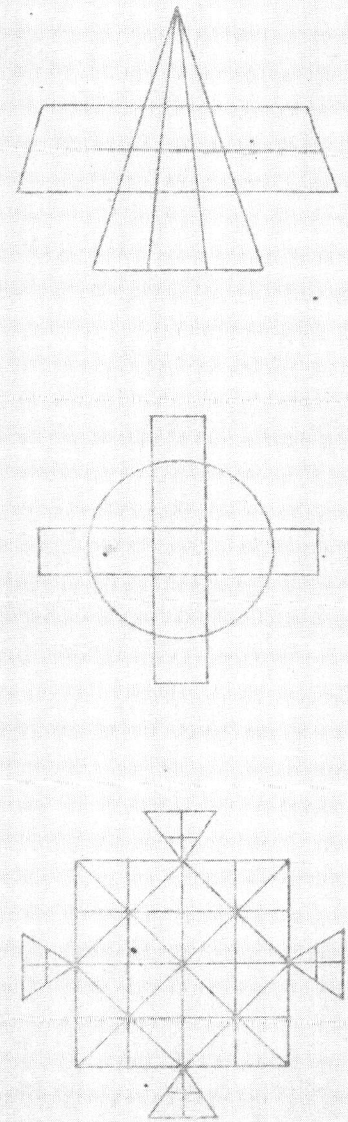

KOTA GAMES

COMPARISON BETWEEN TODAS AND KOTAS.

A comparative table of measurements of Toda and Kota men will be found on page 215. The following summary, based on the averages, will serve, however, to indicate the principal points of difference between male members of the two tribes.

The most obvious distinguishing character is the great development of the hairy system in the Toda, though the Kota frequently has hair well developed on his chest and abdomen. The weight and chest girth of the two tribes are approximately the same, but the mean Toda height is 6·7 cm. greater than that of the Kotas. Corresponding to a greater length of the upper extremities, the span of the arms (*i.e.*, the length from tip to tip of the middle finger with the arms extended at right angles to the body) is 6·7 cm. longer in the Toda than in the Kota, but the difference between height and span is exactly the same (5·4 cm.) in the Toda and Kota. The Todas are broader shouldered than the Kotas, and, though the former do far less manual labour than the latter (many of whom are blacksmiths), their hand grip, as tested by a Salter's dynamometer, is considerably (9 lbs.) greater. The Kotas have broader hips, but a shorter and narrower foot than the Todas. Both Todas and Kotas are dolichocephalic. The cephalic breadth averages the same in the two tribes, but the length of the head is very slightly (·2 cm.) greater in the Toda. The Kota has a wider face with more prominent cheek bones, a greater bimilar breadth, a wider lower jaw, and more developed zygomatic arches. The Toda nose is slightly longer and broader than that of the Kotas. The height from the top of the head (vertex) to the chin is slightly less in the Kota than in the Toda; but corresponding to the greater length from the vertex to the tragus and the more developed frontal region, the facial angle (angle of Cuvier) of the Kota is in excess (3°) of that of the Toda.

The present bulletin is, I trust, only the first of a series giving in detail the results of an anthropological survey of the inhabitants of Southern India, the progress of which must perforce be slow and spasmodic. For the moment I must rest content with merely placing on record the main facts relating to the anthropography and ethnography of the Todas and Kotas, leaving the conclusions to be drawn hereafter, when sufficient material has been collected for the purpose of co-ordination.

NOTE ON KOTA DEATH CEREMONIES.

At the time of writing the foregoing account of the Kotas, I had had no opportunity of witnessing their death ceremonies, and was compelled to base my meagre account thereof on the description given to me by my Kota informant. A few days after my arrival at Kotagiri in the present year, with a view to investigating the Badagas and Irulas, the dismal sound of mourning, to the weird strains of the Kota band, announced that death reigned in the Kota village, and the opportunity was seized to be present as an eye-witness of the ceremonies.

The dead man was a venerable carpenter (No. 3, p. 190) of high position in the community, and the death rites were accordingly carried out on a lavish scale. Soon after daybreak a detachment of villagers hastened to convey the tidings of the death to the Kotas of the neighbouring villages, who arrived on the scene later in the day in Indian file, men in front and women in the rear. As they drew near to the place of mourning, they all, of one accord, commenced the orthodox manifestations of grief, and were met by a deputation of villagers accompanied by the band.

Meanwhile a red flag, tied to the top of a bamboo pole, was hoisted as a signal of death in the village, and a party had gone off to a glade, some two miles distant, to obtain wood for the construction of the funeral car (tēru). The car, when completed, was an elaborate structure, about eighteen feet in height, made of wood and bamboo, in four tiers, each with a canopy of turkey red and yellow cloth, and an upper canopy of white cloth trimmed with red, surmounted by a black umbrella of European manufacture, decorated with red ribbands. The car was profusely adorned throughout with red flags and long white streamers, and with young plantain trees at the base. Tied to the car were a calabash and a bell.

During the construction of the car the corpse remained within the house of the deceased man, outside which the relatives and villagers continued mourning to the dirge-like music of the band, which plays so prominent a part at the death ceremonies of both Todas and Kotas. On the completion of the car, late in the afternoon, it was deposited in front of the house. The corpse dressed up in a coloured turban and gaudy coat as for a nautch party, with a garland of flowers round the neck, and two rupees, a half rupee, and sovereign, gummed on to the forehead, was brought from within the house, lying face upwards on a cot, and placed beneath the lowest canopy of the car. Near the head were placed iron implements and a bag of rice, at the feet a bag of tobacco, and beneath the cot baskets of grain, rice, cakes, &c. The corpse was covered by cloths offered to it as presents, and before it those Kotas who were younger than the dead man prostrated themselves, while those who were older touched the head of the corpse and bowed to it. Around the car the male members of the community executed a wild step-dance, keeping time with the music in the execution of various fantastic movements of the arms and legs.

During the long hours of the night mourning was kept up to the almost incessant music of the band, and the early morn discovered many of the villagers in an advanced stage of intoxication. Throughout the morning dancing round the car was continued by men, sober and inebriated, with brief intervals of rest, and a young buffalo was slaughtered as a matter of routine form, with no special ceremonial, in a pen outside the village, by blows on the back and neck administered with the keen edge of an adze. Towards midday presents of rice from the relatives of the dead man arrived on the back of a pony, which was paraded round the funeral car. From a vessel containing rice and rice water, rice was crammed into the mouths of the near relatives, some of the water poured over their heads, and the remainder offered to the corpse. At intervals a musket, charged with gunpowder, which proved later on a dangerous weapon in the hands of an intoxicated Kota, was let off, and the bell on the car rung.

About 2 P.M., the time announced for the funeral, the cot bearing the corpse, from the forehead of which the coins had been removed, was carried outside the village, followed by the widow and a throng of Kotas of both sexes, young and old, and the car was carried to the foot of the hill, there to await the arrival of the corpse after the performance of various ceremonies. Seated together at some distance from the corpse, the women continued to mourn until the funeral procession was out of sight, those who could not cry spontaneously, or compel the tears to flow, mimicking the expression of woe by contortion of the grief muscles. The most poignant grief was displayed by a man, in a state of extreme intoxication, who sat apart by himself, howling and sobbing, and wound up by creating considerable disturbance at the burning ground. Three young bulls were brought from the village, and led round the corpse. Of these, two were permitted to escape for the time being, while a vain attempt, which would have excited the derision of the expert Toda buffalo catchers, was made by three men hanging on to the head and tail to steer the third bull up to the head of the corpse. The animal, however, proving refractory, it was deemed discreet to put an end to its existence by a blow on the poll with the butt-end of an adze, at some distance from the corpse, which was carried up to it, and made to salute the dead beast's head with the right hand in feeble imitation of the impressive Toda ceremonial. The carcase of the bull was saluted by a few of the Kota men, and subsequently carried off by pariahs.

Supported by females, the exhausted widow of the dead man, who had fainted earlier in the day, was dragged up to the corpse, and, lying back beside it, had to submit to the ordeal of removal of all her jewelry, the heavy brass bangle being hammered off the wrist, supported on a wooden roller, by oft repeated smart blows with mallet and chisel, delivered by a village blacksmith assisted by a besotten individual noted as a consumer of twelve grains of opium daily. The ornaments, as removed, were collected in a basket, to be worn again by the widow after several months.

This revolting ceremony concluded, and a last salutation given by the widow to her dead husband, arches of bamboo were attached to the cot, which was covered over with a coloured table cloth hiding the corpse from sight. A procession was then formed, composed of the corpse on the cot, preceded by the car and musicians, and followed by male Kotas and Badagas, Kota women carrying the baskets of grain and cakes, a vessel containing fire, burning camphor, and, bringing up the rear, a high dignitary of the church, an amateur photographer, and myself. Quickly the procession marched to the burning ground beyond the bazár, situated in a valley by the side of a stream running through a glade in a dense undergrowth of bracken fern and trailing passion-flower. On arrival at the selected spot, a number of agile Kotas swarmed up the sides of the car, and stripped it of its adornments, including the umbrella, and a free fight for the possession of the cloths and flags ensued. The denuded car was then placed over the corpse, which, deprived of all valuable ornaments, and still lying on the cot face upwards, had been meanwhile placed, amid a noisy scene of brawling, on the rapidly constructed funeral pyre. Around the car faggots of fire-wood, supplied, in lieu of wreaths, by different families in the dead man's village, as a tribute of respect to the deceased, were piled up, and the pyre was lighted with torches kindled at a fire which was burning on the ground close by. As soon as the pyre was in a blaze, tobacco, cheroots, cloths, and grain were distributed among those present, and the funeral party dispersed, discussing the events of the day as they returned to their homes, leaving a few men behind in charge of the burning corpse. And peace reigned once more in the Kota village.

A few days later the funeral of an elderly Kota woman took place with a very similar ceremonial. But, suspended from the handle of the umbrella on the top of the car, was a rag doll, which, in appearance, resembled an 'Aunt Sally.'

NOTE ON KOTA ANNUAL FESTIVAL.

The following note is a translation of a description by Dr. Emil Schmidt (Reise nach Süd-Indien, 1894) of the dancing at the Kota annual festival, at which he had the good fortune to be present as an eye-witness :—

"During my stay at Kotagiri the Kotas were celebrating the big festival in honour of their chief god. The feast lasted over twelve days, during which homage was offered to the god every evening, and a dance performed round a fire kept burning near the temple throughout the feast. On the last evening but one, females, as well as males, took part in the dance. As darkness set in, the shrill music, which penetrated to my hotel, attracted me to the Kota village. At the end of the street, which adjoins the back of the temple, a big fire was kept up by continually putting on large long bundles of brushwood. On one side of the fire, close to the flames, stood the musicians with their musical instruments, two hand-drums, a tambourine, beaten by blows on the back, a brass cymbal beaten with a stick, and two pipes resembling oboes. Over and over again the same monotonous tune was repeated by the two latter in quick four-eight time to the accompaniment of the other instruments. On my arrival, about forty male Kotas, young and old, were dancing round the fire, describing a semi-circle, first to one side, then the other, raising the hands, bending the knees, and executing fantastic steps with the feet. The entire circle moved thus slowly forwards, one or the other from time to time giving vent to a spout that sounded like Hau! and, at the conclusion of the dance, there was a general shout all round. Around the circle, partly on the piles of stone near the temple, were seated a number of Kotas of both sexes. A number of Badagas of good position, who had been specially invited to the feast, sat round a small fire on a raised place, which abuts on the back wall of the temple.

"The dance over, the circle of dancers broke up. The drummers held their instruments, rendered damp and lax by the moist evening breeze, so close to the flames that I thought they would get burnt. Soon the music began again to a new tune; first the oboes, and then, as soon as they had got into the proper swing, the other instruments. The melody was not the same as before, but its two movements were repeated without intercession or change. In this dance females, as well as males, took part, grouped in a semi-circle, while the men completed the circle. The men danced boisterously and irregularly. Moving slowly forwards with the entire circle, each dancer turned right round from right to left and from left to right, so that, after every turn, they were facing the fire. The women danced with more precision and more artistically than the men. When they set out on the dance, they first bowed themselves before the fire, and then made left and right half turns with artistic regular steps. Their countenances expressed a mixture of pleasure and embarrassment. None of the dancers wore any special costume, but the women, who were nearly all old and ugly, had, for the most part, a quantity of ornaments in the ears and nose and on the neck, arms and legs.

"In the third dance, played once more in four-eight times, only females took part. It was the most artistic of all, and the slow movements had evidently been well rehearsed beforehand. The various figures consisted of stepping radially to and fro, turning, stepping forwards and backwards, etc., with measured seriousness and solemn dignity. It was for the women, who, at other times, get very little enjoyment, the most important and happiest day in the whole year."

TABLE I.

SUMMARY OF MEASUREMENTS.

TODA MEN.

	Maximum.	Minimum.	Average.	Mean above.	Mean below.	
Weight	135	98	115·4	124·1	105	15 measurements. Average height 168·3 cm.
Hand dynamometer.	100	60	79	87	71	Two men not measured, 112 and 105.
Height	179	159·2	169·6	173·7	164·4	
Height, sitting ...	94·2	82·3	87·9	90	85	
Height, kneeling...	132·8	118·4	124·8	128·6	121	
Height to gladiolus.	136	113	124·4	128·2	121	
Span of arms ...	188·8	164·2	175	180	170·4	
Chest	88·5	77	83	85·7	80·2	
Middle finger to patella.	13	5·9	9	10·7	7·9	16 measurements.
Shoulders	42	37	39·3	40·2	38·5	
Cubit	50·3	43·5	47	48·4	45·4	
Hand, length ...	20	18	18·8	19·1	18·3	
Hand, breadth ...	9·2	7·4	8·1	8·5	7·8	
Middle finger ...	12·7	11	12	12·3	11·6	
Hips	29·2	23·3	25·7	26·6	24·7	
Foot, length ...	27·9	24·2	26·2	27·3	25·4	
Foot, max. breadth.	10·6	8·1	9·2	9·9	8·6	
Cephalic length ...	20	18·3	19·4	19·7	19	
Cephalic breadth.	15·2	13·6	14·2	14·6	13·9	
Cephalic index ...	77·6	69·2	73·3	74	71	

TABLE I—*continued.*

SUMMARY OF MEASUREMENTS—*continued.*

TODA MEN—*continued.*

	Maximum.	Minimum.	Average.	Mean above.	Mean below.
Bigoniac	10·2	8·2	9·6	9·9	9·3
Bizygomatic ...	13·8	12	12·7	13·1	12·5
Maxillo-zygomatic index.	82	67·8	75·7	79·2	73·7
Nasal height ...	5·3	4·5	4·7	4·9	4·6
Nasal breadth ...	4·1	3	3·6	3·8	3·4
Nasal index ...	89·1	61·2	74·9	79·9	70
Vertex to tragus...	14·2	12	13	13·6	12·6
Vertex to chin ...	22·5	19·3	21	21·6	20·3
Facial angle ...	73	62	67	69	65

Note.—In estimating the mean deviation above and below the average, those measurements which were exactly equal to the mean were equally distributed above and below.

The weight is recorded in pounds; the measurements are in centimètres. Excepting where otherwise indicated, it may be understood that the results are based on the examination of twenty-five subjects.

The following average measurements of twenty-five Thiyans belonging to the Malabar Police force are recorded for comparison with those of the Todas :—

	Thiyan.	Toda.
Height	172	169·6
Span of arms	179·6	175
Chest	85·4	83
Shoulders	40·2	39·3
Cubit	48	47
Foot, length	27	26·2

TABLE II.

SUMMARY OF MEASUREMENTS.

TODA WOMEN.

	Maximum.	Minimum.	Average.	Mean above.	Mean below.	
Weight	119·5	84·5	100·5	109·5	91·7	
Height	165·6	146·5	155·6	159·7	151·2	
Height, sitting ...	86·6	76	81·7	83·9	79·7	
Height, kneeling...	122·2	109	114·7	118·5	111·8	
Span of arms ..	172	145	160·8	165·3	156	
Chest (round arm-pits).	86	72	77·7	80·3	75·4	
Shoulders ...	36·5	32·6	34·5	35·1	33·7	
Cubit	47·3	38·9	43·6	45·2	42·7	
Hand, length ...	18·8	16	17·4	17·8	16·8	22 measurements.
Hand, breadth ...	7·8	5·7	7·2	7·5	6·8	
Middle finger ...	11·8	10·3	11·1	11·4	10·9	
Foot, length ...	25·4	21·8	23·8	24·4	23	
Foot, max : breadth.	8·2	6·6	7·6	7·9	7·2	21 measurements.
Cephalic length ...	19·7	17·1	18·4	18·9	17·9	
Cephalic breadth.	14·3	13	13·6	14	13·4	
Cephalic index ...	77·8	70	73·9	75	72·1	
Bigoniac	10	8·7	9·4	9·7	9	
Bizygomatic ...	13	11·5	12·1	12·4	11·7	

Note.—Excepting where otherwise indicated, the results are based on the examination of twenty-five subjects.

TABLE II—*continued.*

SUMMARY OF MEASUREMENTS—*continued.*

TODA WOMEN—*continued.*

	Maximum.	Minimum.	Average.	Mean above.	Mean below.	
Maxillo-zygomatic index.	82·6	74·2	77·4	79·7	75·6	
Nasal height ...	4·9	3·4	4·2	4·5	4	
Nasal breadth ...	3·5	3	3·2	3·3	3·1	
Nasal index ...	91·2	63·3	75·5	78·6	70·9	
Vertex to tragus...	13·8	11·9	12·8	13·3	12·5	
Vertex to chin ...	21·5	18·3	19·7	20·7	18·9	
Facial angle ...	73	61	68	70	66	

TABLE III.

SUMMARY OF MEASUREMENTS.

KOTA MEN.

	Maximum.	Minimum.	Average.	Mean above.	Mean below.	
Weight	147	99·5	115	124	109	20 measurements.
Hand dynamometer.	105	55	70	79	62	
Height	174·2	155	162·9	166·2	158·9	
Height, sitting ...	90·4	82·2	85·8	87·5	83·9	
Height, kneeling...	126·4	112·4	120	122·8	116·4	
Height to gladiolus.	129·2	115	120·6	123·8	118	
Span of arms ...	181·4	155·6	168·3	172	163·7	
Chest	91	77·5	83·3	85·4	81·5	
Middle finger to patella.	13·6	7·4	10·7	11·7	9·2	22 measurements.
Shoulders ...	40·7	34·8	37·7	38·7	36·6	
Cubit	48·6	42·2	45·1	46·2	43·8	
Hand, length ...	19	16·5	18	18·4	17·5	
Hand, breadth ...	8·6	7·4	8	8·3	7·7	
Middle finger ...	12·6	10·7	11·5	11·8	11·2	
Hips	30·4	25·8	27	27·7	26·5	
Foot, length ...	26·3	23·6	25·2	25·7	24·8	
Foot, max. breadth.	9·5	8·1	8·8	9·1	8·5	22 measurements.
Cephalic length ...	20·2	18·3	19·2	19·6	18·8	
Cephalic breadth...	15·1	13·4	14·2	14·5	13·9	
Cephalic index ...	79·1	69·9	74·1	76	72	
Bigoniac ...	10·9	9·1	10·1	10·4	9·8	

TABLE III—*continued.*

SUMMARY OF MEASUREMENTS—*continued.*

KOTA MEN—*continued.*

	Maximum.	Minimum.	Average.	Mean above.	Mean below.	
Bizygomatic ...	13·9	12·1	13	13·3	12·6	
Maxillo-zygomatic index.	85·1	70	77·9	80·4	75·3	
Nasal height ...	5	4·1	4·5	4·7	4·3	
Nasal breadth ...	4	3·1	3·5	3·7	3·3	
Nasal index ...	92·9	64	77·2	83·1	70·5	
Vertex to tragus...	14·9	12·8	13·7	14·2	13·4	
Vertex to chin ...	22·7	19·1	20·8	21·6	19·9	
Facial angle ...	73	66	70	71	69	

Note.—In estimating the mean deviation above and below the average, those measurements which were exactly equal to the mean were equally distributed above and below.

The weight is given in pounds ; the measurements are in centimetres. Excepting where otherwise indicated, the results are based on twenty-five measurements.

TABLE IV.

SUMMARY OF MEASUREMENTS.

KOTA WOMEN.

	Maximum.	Minimum.	Average.	Mean above.	Mean below.	
Weight	97	72	86	90	83	15 measurements.
Height	154·6	138·8	146·3	150·1	142·6	
Height, sitting ...	80·	73·6	77·4	78·9	75·6	
Height, kneeling ...	114·6	103·4	108·3	110·5	105·4	
Span of arms ...	162·2	143·8	151·2	156·1	145·8	19 measurements.
Shoulders ...	35·7	31·1	33·4	34·2	32·5	
Cubit	42·7	37·7	40·2	41·5	39	
Hand, length ...	17·8	16	16·6	17·2	16·3	
Hand, breadth ...	7·8	6·7	7·3	7·6	7·1	
Middle finger ...	11·2	10·2	10·6	10·8	10·4	19 measurements.
Foot, length ...	25	21·3	22·9	23·5	22·3	
Foot, max. breadth.	8·4	7·1	7·7	8·1	7·3	17 measurements.
Cephalic length ...	19·1	17·4	18·2	18·6	17·8	
Cephalic breadth...	14·5	13·1	13·7	14·1	13·3	
Cephalic index ...	79·2	71	74·9	76·9	72·5	
Bigoniac ...	10·3	9	9·4	9·7	9·1	
Bizygomatic ...	12·9	11·7	12·3	12·6	11·9	
Maxillo-zygomatic index.	83·7	70·7	76·8	78·3	74·8	
Nasal height ...	4·8	3·3	4·2	4·4	4	
Nasal breadth ...	3·4	2·9	3·2	3·3	3·1	
Nasal index ...	89·5	70·7	76	80·2	72·1	

TABLE IV—*continued.*

SUMMARY OF MEASUREMENTS—*continued.*

KOTA WOMEN—*continued.*

	Maximum.	Minimum.	Average.	Mean above.	Mean below.	
Vertex to tragus...	13·9	12·2	13·1	13·4	12·9	
Vertex to chin ...	21·5	17·6	19	19·5	18·5	
Facial angle ...	73	68	70	71	69	15 measurements.

Note.—Excepting where otherwise indicated, the results are based on twenty measurements.

TABLE V.

COMPARISON OF MEASUREMENTS.

TODA AND KOTA MEN.

	Todas.	Kotas.
Weight	115·4	115
Height	169·6	162·9
Height, sitting	87·9	85·8
Height, kneeling	124·8	120
Height to gladiolus	124·4	120·6
Span of arms	175	168·3
Chest	83	83·3
Middle finger to patella	9	10·7
Shoulders	39·3	37·7
Cubit	47	45·1
Hand, length	18·8	18
Hand, breadth	8·1	8
Middle finger	12	11·5
Hips	25·7	27
Foot, length	26·2	25·2
Foot, breadth	9·2	8·8
Cephalic length	19·4	19·2
Cephalic breadth	14·2	14·2
Cephalic index	73·3	74·1
Bigoniac	9·6	10·1
Bizygomatic	12·7	13

TABLE V—*continued.*

COMPARISON OF MEASUREMENTS—*continued.*

TODA AND KOTA MEN—*continued.*

	Todas.	Kotas.
Maxillo-zygomatic index	75·7	77·9
Nasal height	4·7	4·5
Nasal breadth	3·6	3·5
Nasal index	74·9	77·2
Vertex to tragus	13	13·7
Vertex to chin	21	20·8
Facial angle	67	70

THE BRÁHMANS, KAMMÁLANS, PALLIS, AND PARIAHS OF MADRAS CITY.

LOOKING at the table on page 230, I picture to myself the sad feelings of a candidate at an examination in anthropology, overflowing with parrot knowledge of his text books, on being presented with the following examination paper:—

Saturday, 20th January, 2 to 5 P.M.

ANTHROPOLOGY.

Draw such conclusions as you are able from the figures in the table supplied.

The table, based on measurements recorded by myself, affords fitting material for an essay on comparative anthropology, and, reverting for once to the position of candidate, I will answer, in my own way, the question set by myself as examiner.

At first sight a complicated jumble of figures, the table resolves itself naturally into three primary groups, viz:—

1. Todas of the Nilgiris, above middle height (170 to 165 cm.), with a difference of only 5·4 cm. between the span of the arms and height, a distance of 9 cm. from the middle finger to the patella, a head conspicuously long in proportion to its breadth, and long, narrow nose.

2. Bráhmans, Kammálans, Pallis, and Pariahs below middle height (165 to 160 cm.) with a difference between the span of the arms and height ranging from 11·4 to 9·4 cm., the distance from middle finger to patella varying between 8·4 and 10·1 cm., and a nasal index ranging from 77·2 to 84·5.

3. Paniyans of the Wynád, of low stature, with a difference of 7·8 cm. between the span of the arms and height, a distance of 7·3 cm. from middle finger to patella, a long hand, and broad, short nose with a very high nasal index (95·1).

In placing the Kammálans as "below middle height," I give them the benefit of the three millimetres below the minimum (160 cm.), as they should be sharply separated from the various people (Muppas, Cherumans, Kurumans,

Paniyans, &c.), whose mean height is uniformly between 157 and 158 cm.

With the Todas I have already dealt in detail. With the Paniyans I shall deal in like manner hereafter. Suffice it, for the moment, to state that they are a short, curly (not wooly) headed, broad-nosed people, inhabiting the Wynád and plains of Malabar, who are popularly believed (with no evidence in support of the belief) to be of African descent. In the present essay I shall confine myself mainly to a consideration of the Bráhmans belonging to the poorer classes, Kammálans, Pallis, and Pariahs of Madras city, based, in each case, on measurements of forty adult men, varying in age from twenty-five to forty, and taken at random.

It may be contended that it is not possible to arrive at an average, in the case of a large community, such, for example, as the Bráhmans, by measurement of so few individuals as forty. I, therefore, produce in evidence of the fairness of the figures recorded in table VI, table VII, in which the mean measurements, as estimated after ten, twenty, thirty, and forty measurements, are givén. The results show, in a very marked manner, that each series of ten individuals conformed, as regards weight and measurements of the head, trunk, and extremities, to the same type. More especially would I invite attention to the measurements of the height, head, and nose. Taking some of the more important factors in table VII, and examining the greatest deviation from the averages, the results are as follows :—

	Greatest deviation. 2·5 cm. = 1 inch. 1 mm. = ·1 cm.
Height	1·1 cm.
Span of arms	1·3 ,,
Hand, length	3 mm.
Foot, length	2 ,,
Cephalic length	1 ,,
Cephalic breadth	1 ,,
Nasal height	1 ,,
Nasal breadth	1 ,,

The Bráhmans, who returned themselves as Mádhava, Smarta, Sóliya, and Vaishnava, belonged to the classes of agriculturist, clerk, gurú, mendicant, and schoolmaster.

The Kammálans comprised blacksmiths, carpenters, stonemasons, and goldsmiths; the Pallis, cultivators, fitters, gardeners, hand-cart draggers, masons, polishers, and sawyers;

the Pariahs, coachmen, coolies, dressing-boys, fish-sellers, gardeners, and horse-keepers.

It would be impossible, within the limits of a single, essay, to deal at length with the "manners and customs," history, religion, &c., of the Bráhmans, Kammálans, Pallis, and Pariahs: and I cannot do better than reproduce the epitomes contained in my constant companion, the Madras Census Report, 1891, wherein Mr. H. A. Stuart has brought together, for the benefit of the anthropologist, a vast store of information, both statistical and general.

1. BRÁHMANS.

"It has often been asserted, and is now the general belief of ethnologists, that the Bráhmans of the South are not pure Aryans, but are a mixed Aryan and Dravidian race. In the earliest times the caste division was much less rigid than now, and a person of another caste could become a Bráhman by attaining the Bráhmanical standard of knowledge, and assuming Bráhmanical functions. And, when we see Nambúdiri Bráhmans even at the present day contracting alliances, informal though they be, with the women of the country, it is not difficult to believe that, on their first arrival, such unions were even more common, and that the children born of them would be recognised as Bráhmans, though perhaps regarded as an inferior class. However, those Bráhmans, in whose veins the mixed blood is supposed to run, are even to this day regarded as lower in the social scale, and are not allowed to mix freely with the pure Bráhman community."

2. KAMMÁLANS.

"The name Kammála is a generic term applied to the five artisan castes, viz., (1) Tattán or Kamsala (goldsmith); (2) Kannán or Kanchara (brazier); (3) Kollan or Kammara (blacksmith); (4) Tac'chan or Vadra (carpenter); and (5) Kal Tac'chan or Silpi (stone-mason). The Kammálas assert that they are descended from Visvakarma, the architect of the

30

gods, and, in many parts of the country, they claim to be equal with the Bráhmans, calling themselves Visva Bráhmans. . . . . Inscriptions show that, as late as the year 1033 A.D., the Kammálans were treated as a very inferior caste, for they, like the Paraiyans, Pallans, &c., were confined to a particular part or *chéri* of the village site. . . . The five main sub-divisions of the Kammálans do not generally intermarry. They have priests of their own, and do not allow even Bráhmans to officiate for them, but they imitate the Bráhmans in their ceremonies. Girls must be married before puberty, and widow re-marriage is strictly prohibited. The use of flesh and alcohol is also nominally forbidden. Many of them bury the dead in a sitting posture, but cremation is also practised. Their usual title is Áchári, and some call themselves *Pattan*, which is the equivalent of the Bráhman Bhatta. To this account may be added the fact that the Kammálans wear the sacred thread."

3. PALLIS.

"The Pallis, Vanniyans, or Padaiyáchis, are found in all the Tamil districts . . . . That the Pallis were once an influential and independent community may be admitted, and, in their present desire to be classed as Kshatriyas, they are merely giving expression to their belief, but, unless an entirely new meaning is given to the term 'Kshatriya,' their claim must be dismissed as absurd. After the fall of the Pallava dynasty the Pallis became agricultural servants under the Vallálas, and it is only since the advent of British rule that they have begun to assert their claims to a higher position. The bulk of them are still labourers, but many now farm their own lands, while others are engaged in trade.

"They do not wear the sacred thread. Some of them engage Bráhmans to officiate as their priests. Their girls are usually married after they attain maturity. The re-marriage of widows is permitted, and actually practised. Divorce is said to be permitted only in case of adultery by the wife, but this statement requires confirmation. They both burn and bury the dead. Their usual agnomen is Kavandan or Padaiyáchi, but some of them, who strive for a higher social standing, call themselves 'Náyakkan.'"

4. PARIAHS.

"The Paraiyan or Pariah caste of the Tamil country numbers, according to the census, over two million souls. . . . . The tribe must at one time have held an influential position, for there are curious survivals of this in certain privileges which Paraiyans have retained to the present day. I quote the following remarks of Mr. Walhouse on this subject :—

"'It is well known that the servile castes in Southern India once held far higher positions, and were indeed masters of the land on the arrival of the Bráhmanical caste. Many curious vestiges of their ancient power still survive in the shape of certain privileges, which are jealously cherished, and, their origin being forgotten, are misunderstood. These privileges are remarkable instances of survivals from an extinct order of society. Shadows of long-departed supremacy, bearing witness to a period when the present haughty high-caste races were suppliants before the ancestors of degraded classes, whose touch is now regarded as pollution. At Mélkotta, the chief seat of the followers of Rámánuja-áchárya, and at the Bráhman temple at Bailur, the Holeyars or Pareyars have the right of entering the temple on three days in the year, specially set apart for them. . . . In the great festival of Siva at Tiruválúr in Tanjore, the headman of the Pareyars is mounted on the elephant with the god, and carries his *chauri*. In Madras, at the annual festival of the goddess of Black Town, when a *táli* is tied round the neck of the idol in the name of the entire community, a Pareyar is chosen to represent the bridegroom.'

"'The Paraiyans have been but little affected by Bráhmanical doctrines and customs, though in respect to ceremonies they have not escaped their influence. Paraiyans are nominally Saivities, but in reality they are demon-worshippers. The Valluvas are their priests. The marriage of girls before puberty is very rare. Divorce is easy; a husband can send his wife away at will, and she on her part can dissolve the marriage tie by simply returning the *táli*. In such cases the husband takes the children, or contributes for their maintenance. Widow marriage is freely allowed. The dead are usually buried.'"

Turning now to a detailed analysis of the figures in table VI, with more special reference to the Bráhmans,

Kammálans, Pallis, and Pariahs. The Bráhmans are the best nourished, as indicated by the weights, which, relative to stature = 100, are as follows:—Bráhmans 70·8; Pariahs 65·4; Pallis 64·4; Kammálans 62·9 lbs. In height the Bráhmans, Pallis, and Pariahs are very closely allied, and differentiated from the Kammálans, as shown by the following table [20]:—

	Average.	Mean above.	Mean below.
Bráhmans	162·5	167·9	157·1
Pallis	162·5	166·7	157·5
Pariahs	162·1	166·3	157·4
Kammálans	159·7	164·1	155·2

The relative lengths of the upper extremities are best determined by a comparison of the *grande envergure* (span of arms) with the height, and of the distance from the middle finger to the patella.

The difference between the span of the arms and height ranges between 10 cm. and 10·8 cm. in the Bráhmans, Pallis, and Pariahs, and is over 11 cm. in the Kammálans; or, expressed relatively to stature = 100, and compared with the averages of English and Negroes, the results are as follows:—

English	104·4
Pariahs	106·2
Pallis	106·2
Bráhmans	106·6
Kammálans	107·1
Negroes	108·1

The results, then, in the classes under review, range between those of the English and Negroes, of whom the latter, owing to the great length of the upper extremities, have a very wide span.

The distance from the tip of the middle finger to the top of the patella (the extensor muscles of the thigh being

[20] In this and subsequent tables the measurements are recorded in centimetres.

relaxed) diminishes as the length of the upper extremities is greater. It is greatest in the Bráhmans, least in the Kammálans, and intermediate (and, as in the case of the span, the same) in the Pallis and Pariahs. The following table gives the results, relative to stature=100, as compared with the results of measurement of American soldiers, Negroes, and the Paniyans of the Wynád :—

American soldiers	7·5
Bráhmans	6·2
Pallis	5·8
Pariahs	5·8
Kammálans	5·3
Paniyans	4·6
Negroes	4·4

As in the case of the difference between span and height, the classes under review come between the white men and the Negroes, to the latter of whom the short, broad-nosed Paniyans approximate most closely.

Once again, the length of the hand is practically the same in the Pallis and Pariahs, who come between the long-handed Bráhmans and short-handed Kammálans. But, in length of foot, the Bráhmans and Pariahs (whose average foot-length is practically the same) exceed the Pallis and Kammálans. A long hand or foot, it may be noted, *en passant*, is not considered a characteristic of inferiority.

I take this opportunity of correcting an error in Topinard's 'Anthropology,' based on the rough tape measurements of Dr. Shortt, to the effect that the Toda foot is "monstrously large," viz., 18·1 relative to stature = 100. My measurements were made with a sliding scale on twenty-five Toda men taken at random, and gave the following results :—

	Maximum.	Minimum.	Average.	Mean above.	Mean below.
Actual	27·9	24·2	26·2	27·3	25·4
Relative to stature=100.	16·9	14·6	15·4	16	15·1

So far, then, from the length of the Toda foot being monstrously large, it is, as shown by the following table, shorter, relative to stature, than that of all, except one, of the classes or tribes of Southern India, whose investigation I have, up to the present time, completed :—

	Height.	Length of foot.	Length of foot relative to stature =100.
Kongas	159	25·5	16·1
Kammálans	159·7	25·1	16
Pariahs	162·1	26	16
Bráhmans	162·5	25·9	15·9
Paniyans	157·4	25	15·9
Cherumans	157·5	24·7	15·7
Pallis	162·5	25·5	15·7
Irulas	159·8	24·9	15·6
Muppas	157·7	24·5	15·5
Kotas	162·9	25·2	15·5
Todas	169·6	26·2	15·4
Badagas	164·1	25	15·2

Though not included in table VI, the relation of the breadth of the hips, across the spines of the ilia, to the length of the foot, appears to me to serve as a distinguishing characteristic between different races, castes, and tribes. I, therefore, reproduce the results so far as my investigations permit :—

	Foot length.	Hips breadth.	Foot.	Hips.
Kotas	25·2	27		+ 1·8
Badagas	25	26·6	...	+ 1·6
Irulas ...	24·9	25·4		+ ·5
Bráhmans	25·9	26		+ ·1
Kongas ...	25·5	25·6		+ ·1
Paniyans	25	24·3	+ ·7	
Todas	26·2	25·7	+ ·5	
Cherumans	24·7	24·2	+ ·5	
Muppas	24·5	24·1	+ ·4	...
Pariahs	26	25·9	+ ·1	...
Kammálans	25·1	25·1	– 0	– 0
Pallis	25·5	25·5	– 0	– 0

This table shows that, in the classes under review, and in the Kongas, the breadth of the hips and length of the foot are practically equal, whereas in the Badagas, Kotas, and Irulas the length of the foot is appreciably shorter, and in the Todas, Paniyans, Cherumans, and Muppas, longer than the breadth of hips.

Passing on to a consideration of the measurements of the head, it may be stated at the outset that the Bráhmans are separated, not only from the Kammálans, Pallis, and Pariahs, but also, as shown in the following table, from all the other classes or tribes of Southern India which I have as yet investigated, with the exception of the Kongas of Coimbatore, by the relation of the maximum transverse diameter to the maximum antero-posterior diameter of the head (cephalic index). Though the cephalic index of the Kongas is slightly greater, the mean length and breadth of their heads are considerably less than those of the Bráhmans, being only 17·8 cm. and 13·7 cm. against 18·6 cm. and 14·2 cm.

	Maximum.	Minimum.	Average.	Mean above.	Mean below.
Badagas	77·5	66·1	71·7	73·9	69·5
Muppas	77·1	62·3	72·3	74·5	70·3
Pallis	80	64·4	73	75·5	70·1
Todas	77·6	69·2	73·3	74	71
Pariahs	78·3	64·8	73·6	75·5	71·4
Cherumans	80·1	67·7	73·9	76·3	71·7
Paniyans	81·1	69·4	74	76·3	72
Kotas	79·1	69·9	74·1	76	72
Kammálans	81·5	68·4	75	77·8	72·2
Irulas	80·9	70·8	75·8	78	73·8
Bráhmans	84	69	76·5	78·9	73·6
Kongas	81·7	70	77	78·2	74·2

The results of measurements of the length of the head of Bráhmans, Kammálans, Pallis, and Pariahs show that the average length is the same in all except the Kammálans, in whom it is slightly (·2 cm.) shorter.

CEPHALIC LENGTH.

	Maximum.	Minimum.	Average.	Mean above.	Mean below.
Bráhmans	19·9	17·3	18·6	19·1	18·2
Kammálans	19·7	17·3	18·4	18·9	17·8
Pallis	19·6	17·4	18·6	19	18·2
Pariahs	19·7	17	18·6	19·1	18·2

The results of measurement of the breadth of the head, on the other hand, show that the average breadth of the Bráhman head is considerably in excess of that of the Kammálans, Pallis, and Pariahs.

CEPHALIC BREADTH.

	Maximum.	Minimum.	Average.	Mean above.	Mean below.
Bráhmans	15·2	12·7	14·2	14·6	13·7
Kammálans	14·7	13·1	13·7	14	13·4
Pallis	14·6	12·1	13·6	14	13·2
Pariahs	14·5	13	13·7	14	13·4

The great breadth of the Bráhman head, in comparison with that of the other three classes, is well brought out by the following table, which gives the number of times in which the head of members of each class measured between 12 and 13, 13 and 14, 14 and 15, and 15 and 16 centimetres respectively :—

	12–13	13–14	14 15	15–16	Total.
Bráhmans	1	9	27	3	40
Kammálans	1	22	17	...	40
Pallis	3	30	7	...	40
Pariahs	..	27	13	...	40

The mean measurements of the nose of the Bráhmans, Kammálans, Pallis, and Pariahs, which are summed up in the following tables, and compared with those of the typical broad-nosed Paniyans, show that in all, except the Paniyans, the average breadth of the nose is the same, but the length is slightly greatest in the Bráhmans, and least in the Pariahs. A Bráhman school-master was the possessor of the longest nose (5·5 cm.), and a Pariah dressing-boy of the broadest (4·5 cm.). But, in the course of my investigation, I came across many dark-skinned Bráhmans, with high nasal index, with whom I for one should be sorry to claim Aryan kinship. More especially have I in mind a swarthy individual with a nose 4·1 cm. × 3·9 cm. and, for a Bráhman, a monstrous nasal index of 95·1.

NASAL HEIGHT.

	Maximum.	Minimum.	Average.	Mean above.	Mean below.
Bráhmans	5·5	4·1	4·7	4·9	4·4
Kammálans	5·2	4·1	4·6	4·8	4·3
Pallis	5·1	4·1	4·6	4·8	4·4
Pariahs	5·1	4·1	4·5	4·8	4·3
Paniyans	4·8	3·3	4	4·2	3·7

NASAL BREADTH.

	Maximum.	Minimum.	Average.	Mean above.	Mean below.
Bráhmans	3·9	3	3·6	3·7	3·4
Kammálans	4	3·1	3·6	3·8	3·4
Pallis	4·1	3·1	3·6	3·8	3·4
Pariahs	4·5	3·1	3·6	3·8	3·4
Paniyans	4·2	3·2	3·8	4	3·6

NASAL INDEX.

	Maximum.	Minimum.	Average.	Mean above.	Mean below.
Bráhmans	95·1	60	76·7	82·2	71·6
Kammálans	90·9	63·3	77·3	82·6	72·5
Pallis	95·9	60·8	77·9	83·5	73·3
Pariahs	91·8	66	80	86	74·3
Paniyans	108·6	72·9	95·1	100·9	88·2

To sum up in a few words the distinguishing characteristics of Bráhmans, Kammálans, Pallis, and Pariahs, as deduced from the measurements. The Bráhmans are characterised by the greatest weight, greatest breadth of head, greatest distance from the middle finger to the patella, and the longest hand. The Kammálans are at once separated from the other three classes by shortness of stature, hand, and foot; and the Pallis and Pariahs are connected together by the close relation of their weight, height, difference between span and height, distance from the middle finger to the patella, and length of hand.

It must not for a moment be supposed that the present note is intended to be a final summing up of the characteristics, deduced from anthropometric observations, of the Bráhmans of Southern India. Rather does it represent the initial stage of an enquiry, in carrying out which I foresee difficulties resulting from dread of pollution by my instruments, especially the goniometer, which has to be held between the teeth when the facial angle is being determined.

Anthropological research among uneducated and superstitious people who believe in the efficacy of a thread in warding off the evil influence of devils, and are incapable of appreciating that one's motive is quite harmless, requires tact, bribery, coaxing, and a large store of patience. Last year, for example, the Paniyan women believed that I was going to have the finest specimens among them stuffed for the Madras Museum, and the Muppas of the Wynád were afraid that I was a recruiting sergeant, bent on enlisting the strongest men of their community for a native Malabar army; and, in a recent wandering on the lower slopes of the Nílgiris, a man who was 'wanted' for some mild crime of ancient date, came to be measured, but absolutely refused to submit to the operation on the plea that he was afraid that the height measuring standard was the gallows. Nor would he permit me to take his photograph lest it should be used for the purpose of criminal identification.

TABLE VI.

	Weight.	Height.	Difference between span and height.	Middle finger to patella.	Hand, length.	Foot, length.	Cephalic length.	Cephalic breadth.	Nasal height.	Nasal breadth.	Nasal index.
	LBS.	CM.	CM.	CM.	CM.	CM.	CM.	CM.	CM.	CM.	
Todas	115·4	169·6	5·4	9	18·8	26·2	19·4	14·2	4·7	3·6	74·9
Bráhmans	115	162·5	10·8	10·1	18·3	25·9	18·6	14·2	4·7	3·6	77·2
Kammálans	100·4	159·7	11·3	8·4	17·6	25·1	18·4	13·7	4·6	3·6	76·2
Pallis	104·6	162·5	10·1	9·5	17·9	25·5	18·6	13·6	4·6	3·6	77·9
Pariahs	106	162·1	10	9·4	17·9	26	18·6	13·7	4·5	3·6	80
Paniyans	99·6	157·4	7·8	7·3	18·5	25	18·4	13·6	4	3·8	95·1

TABLE VII.

BRÂHMANS.

(AVERAGES OF TEN, TWENTY, THIRTY AND FORTY MEASUREMENTS).

—	10	20	30	40
Weight	114·9	115·7	115	115
Height	163·3	163·6	162·3	162·5
Height, sitting	85·1	85·4	85·2	85·4
Height, kneeling	119·5	119·8	118·9	119·2
Height to gladiolus	121·8	122·4	121·6	122·1
Span of arms	174·6	173·4	172·9	173·3
Middle finger to patella	9·6	10·8	10·4	10·1
Shoulders	39·6	39·2	39·2	39·3
Cubit	46·5	46·1	45·9	46
Hand, length	18·4	18·2	18·1	18·3
Hand, breadth	8	8	8	8
Middle finger	11·7	11·5	11·5	11·6
Hips	25·8	25·7	25·9	26
Foot, length	26·1	26·1	25·9	25·9
Foot, breadth	8·5	8·7	8·7	8·7
Cephalic length	18·7	18·7	18·6	18·6
Cephalic breadth	14·2	14·3	14·2	14·2
Cephalic index	75·9	76·2	76·4	76·4
Bigoniac	10·2	10·1	10	10
Bizygomatic	12·8	12·9	12·9	12·9
Maxillo-zygomatic index	80	77·9	77·7	77·7
Nasal height	4·6	4·7	4·7	4·7
Nasal breadth	3·7	3·6	3·6	3·6
Nasal index	78·6	77·3	77·2	77·2
Vertex to tragus	14	14	14	14·1
Vertex to chin	20·8	20·8	20·7	20·9
Facial angle	68	69	68	69

Note.—In this and the following tables the weight is recorded in pounds; the measurements are in centimetres. The results are based in each table on the measurement of forty subjects.

TABLE VIII.

SUMMARY OF MEASUREMENTS.

BRÁHMANS.

—	Max.	Min.	Average.	Mean above	Mean below
Weight	161	90	115	132	107
Height	174·6	153	169·5	167·9	157·1
Height, sitting	90·8	81	85·4	87·8	83·2
Height, kneeling	127·8	108·2	119·2	122·9	115·7
Height to gladiolus	133·6	112·6	122·1	126·2	117·9
Span of arms	187·8	160	173·3	180	166·7
Chest	98	70	81	85·6	77·1
Middle finger to patella ...	14·8	4·8	10·1	12·1	8·5
Shoulders	43·7	34·6	39·3	41·3	34·2
Cubit	49·9	41·6	46	47·8	44·3
Hand, length	19·8	16·1	18·3	19·1	17·5
Hand, breadth	9·1	7·2	8	8·4	7·7
Middle finger	12·6	10·7	11·6	12	11·2
Hips	30·3	23	26	27·6	24·9
Foot, length	28·8	22·2	25·9	26·8	24·7
Foot, breadth	9·8	7·7	8·7	9·1	8·2
Cephalic length	19·9	17·3	18·6	19·1	18·2
Cephalic breadth	15·2	12·7	14·2	14·6	13·7
Cephalic index	84	69	76·5	78·9	73·6
Bigoniac	11·1	9	10	10·4	9·5
Bizygomatic	14·1	11·6	12·9	13·3	12·4
Maxillo-zygomatic index. ...	91·5	69·5	77·7	81·1	74·9
Nasal height	5·5	4·1	4·7	4·9	4·4
Nasal breadth	3·9	3	3·6	3·7	3·4
Nasal index	95·1	60	76·7	82·2	71·6
Vertex to tragus	14·7	12·8	14·1	14·5	13·5
Vertex to chin	22·9	18·1	20·9	21·5	20·2
Facial angle	74	61	69	71	66

TABLE IX.

SUMMARY OF MEASUREMENTS.

KAMMÁLANS.

—	Max.	Min.	Average.	Mean above	Mean below
Weight	130	79	100·4	111·5	92·2
Height	171·8	146·4	159·7	164·1	155·2
Height, sitting	88	75·6	82·5	84·4	80
Height, kneeling	126·2	107·2	117·4	120·3	114·3
Height to gladiolus ...	129·8	111·2	120	123·6	116·8
Span of arms	188·4	158·8	171	175·5	167
Chest	86	71	78	81·4	75·5
Middle finger to patella ...	13·4	4·2	8·4	10·6	6·8
Shoulders	42·8	36	39·2	40·7	38
Cubit	50·6	42·2	46·2	47·5	45
Hand, length	19	16·2	17·6	18·3	17·1
Hand, breadth	8·9	7·4	8·1	8·4	7·9
Middle finger	12·5	10·7	11·4	11·8	11·1
Hips	29	23·2	25·1	26·1	223·4
Foot, length	27·2	23·2	25·1	26·2	4·2
Foot, breadth	9·7	7·8	8·6	9	8·3
Cephalic length	19·7	17·3	18·4	18·9	17·8
Cephalic breadth	14·7	13·1	13·7	14	413·
Cephalic index	81·5	68·4	75	77·8	72·2
Bigoniac	11·1	8·6	9·7	10·3	9·2
Bizygomatic	13·3	11·6	12·7	13	12·4
Maxillo-zygomatic index ...	85·3	69·5	76·2	79·6	73·6
Nasal height	5·2	4·1	4·6	4·8	4·3
Nasal breadth	4	3·1	3·6	3·8	3·4
Nasal index	90·9	63·3	77·3	82·6	72·5
Vertex to tragus	14·6	12·7	13·7	14·1	13·4
Vertex to chin	22·9	18·3	20·9	21·7	19·8
Facial angle	75	64	70	72	68

TABLE X.

SUMMARY OF MEASUREMENTS.

PALLIS.

—	Max.	Min.	Aver-age.	Mean above	Mean below
Weight	123	85	104·6	111·6	96
Height	169·4	151	162·5	166·7	157·5
Height, sitting	89·5	77·9	83·6	85·4	81·8
Height, kneeling	123·8	111	118·8	121·5	115·8
Height to gladiolus	128·8	114	121·5	125·9	117·8
Span of arms. ...	182·2	159·6	172·6	177·6	167·9
Chest	85·5	72	79·2	81·8	76·3
Middle finger to patella ...	14·2	4·2	9·5	11·1	7·7
Shoulders	41·9	36·2	39·4	40·6	38·2
Cubit	49·3	41·6	46·2	47·7	44·6
Hand, length	19·7	16	17·9	18·7	17·1
Hand, breadth	8·9	7·4	8·1	8·4	7·7
Middle finger	12·1	10	11·4	11·8	10·9
Hips	27·3	24	25·5	26·5	24·6
Foot, length	27·6	23·3	25·5	26·4	24·6
Foot, breadth	10	7·8	8·9	9·3	8·4
Cephalic length	19·6	17·4	18·6	19	18·2
Cephalic breadth	14·6	12·1	13·6	14	13·2
Cephalic index	80	64·4	73	75·5	70·1
Bigoniac	10·8	9	9·9	10·3	9·5
Bizygomatic	13·6	11·9	12·7	13·1	12·3
Maxillo-zygomatic index ...	85·7	72·4	78	80·1	76
Nasal height	5·1	4·1	4·6	4·8	4·4
Nasal breadth	4·1	3·1	3·6	3·8	3·4
Nasal index	95·1	60·8	77·9	83·5	73·3
Vertex to tragus	14·6	12·5	13·8	14·2	13·4
Vertex to chin	22·5	19·3	21·1	21·7	20·7
Facial angle	76	63	69	71	64

TABLE XI.

SUMMARY OF MEASUREMENTS.

PARIAHS.

—	Max.	Min.	Average.	Mean above	Mean below
Weight	128	91	106	114	99
Height	171·4	149·4	162·1	166·3	157·4
Height, sitting	89·9	76	84·5	86·8	82·7
Height, kneeling	127·2	109·4	119·4	122·7	116·4
Height to gladiolus	129·6	112·5	122·4	125·5	119
Span of arms	186·6	159·8	172·1	178	167·2
Chest	84·5	74·5	79·3	81·6	77·6
Middle finger to patella. ...	14	5·5	9·4	11·2	7·8
Shoulders	41·4	36·8	39·4	40·4	38·6
Cubit	49·7	42·5	46·1	47·7	44·9
Hand, length	19·6	15·5	17·9	18·5	17·3
Hand, breadth	8·8	7·4	8	8·3	7·9
Middle finger	12·9	10·4	11·4	11·7	11·1
Hips	28·2	24·1	25·9	26·8	25
Foot, length	28·8	24·2	26	26·9	25·2
Foot, breadth	10	8·1	9·1	9·5	8·7
Cephalic length	19·7	17	18·6	19·1	18·1
Cephalic breadth ...	14·5	13	13·7	14	13·4
Cephalic index	78·3	64·8	73·6	75·5	71·4
Bigoniac	11·1	9·1	10	10·5	9·5
Bizygomatic	13·7	12·2	12·9	13·2	12·6
Maxillo-zygomatic index. ...	84·7	67·4	77·6	81·3	74·8
Nasal height	5·1	4·1	4·5	4·8	4·3
Nasal breadth	4·5	3·1	3·6	3·8	3·4
Nasal index	91·8	66	80	86	74·3
Vertex to tragus	14·9	12·9	13·8	14·2	13·4
Vertex to chin	23·2	19	21·3	22	20·6
Facial angle	75	62	68	71	66